Blue Ribbon Bow

A Fly-Fishing History of the Bow River—
Canada's Greatest Trout Stream

Jim McLennan

Blue Ribbon Books

JOHNSON GORMAN PUBLISHERS

The Publishers
Johnson Gorman Publishers
3669 - 41 Avenue
Red Deer Alberta Canada T4N 2X7

Credits
Cover design by Cat Tail Publishing.
Text design by Full Court Press.
Maps and illustrations by David Soltess.
Front cover photographs softcover and hardcover editions: *top* Jim
    McLennan, *lower right* Lynda McLennan, *lower center* Jim
    McLennan, *lower left* Bob Scammell.
Back cover photographs softcover edition: *top* Lynda McLennan,
    center Barry Mitchell, *bottom* Jim McLennan.
Back cover photographs hardcover edition: *top left* Lynda McLen-
    nan, *center left* Barry Mitchell, *bottom left* Jim McLennan, *right*
    Barry Mitchell. Author photograph Lynda McLennan.
Photographs pages: 169-184 *top* by Jim and Lynda McLennan.
Photograph page 184 *bottom* by Bob Scammell.
The publishers gratefully acknowledge the Provincial Archives of
Alberta for the following photographs: A.453, A.11094, A.1345,
A.2658, A.5279, A.8127, B.123, B.9661, B.9644, B.1960, B.2428,
B.9604, B.2411, B.2396, B.9624, B.1835, B.3175, B1.1001/2, G.2182,
P.129, P.3430, P.3414, P4740, J.1378/1.
Printed and bound in Canada by Friesens for Johnson Gorman
Publishers.

5 4 3 2 1

Financial support provided by the Alberta Foundation for the
Arts, a beneficiary of the Lottery Fund of the Government of
Alberta.

COMMITTED TO THE DEVELOPMENT OF CULTURE AND THE ARTS

Canadian Cataloguing in Publication Data
McLennan, Jim, 1953–
Blue ribbon Bow
ISBN 0-921835-50-7 (bound)—ISBN 0-921835-51-5 (pbk.)
1. Trout fishing—Alberta—Bow River. 2. Fly fishing—Alberta—
Bow River. 3. Bow River (Alta.)—Description and travel. 1. Title.
SH688.C3M34 1998 799.1'757'0971233 C99-910100-5

To the memory of Bill Griffiths, biologist and fly-fisher. Today's Bow River anglers will be forever indebted to Bill.

Contents

Foreword

JIM MCLENNAN'S RIVER is a big one: the Bow runs nearly 400 miles (640 km) from beneath the peaks of Banff National Park, through a great city and across pasture and farmland. Some of its waters eventually reach Hudson Bay.

McLennan has watched his river run through his years as a river guide, when there were great, lonely reaches, through the boom that made Calgary a great river city and through times when ceaseless grasping for water threatened the Bow, its trout, its gliding pools and its scenic seasons.

McLennan accepts the river's moods with smiling tolerance, and when the wind blows upstream he rows his laden johnboat with cheerful enthusiasm, apparently recalling the days of happy breezes, when he simply steered and watched trout flashes as they took streamers or dry flies.

Most of Canada is no arctic wilderness but stateside anglers still feel a little of the awe that has always been a part of the Northland, and the Bow, with its origins beneath snowy peaks, fits the design. There is the childish feeling that the red-coated Mounted Police in Calgary are actually guarding the huge and mysterious North.

Traveling anglers generally think of the Bow as a drift river, and the aluminum johnboats share the scene with more colorful high-end driftboats, while a parking lot may have an expensive cartopped canoe, handmade with exotic materials and care.

McLennan's book is much more than a guide's guide to a fishing stream. A fly-fishing addict, he has forgotten none of what he learned as a youthful guide and drifts as a master angler, naturalist and protective conservationist with the uncanny ability to see a distant pod of rising fish. Much of his life has been lived with his river, and he explains his good old days briefly and then addresses the river that is and will be. He meets the continuing boom of Calgary and the rest of Canada as development must be met near all rising trout, but he points out that the Bow is the only big trout stream that flows through a really large city and still produces.

Most of the world's trout anglers would be happy to claim the Bow. McLennan's photos of the Bow in fall come very close to being all trout rivers in fall, and the Bow winter scene is really all trout rivers in winter.

–Charles F. Waterman
Deland, Florida

Author's
Acknowledgments

MANY PEOPLE aided in the production of this book. The order in which their names appear is not a rating of the importance of their contributions. I wish to thank Grant Kennedy and Lone Pine Publishing for having the initial idea of producing a book on the Bow River back in the 1980s. Special thanks are due the Bow River Chapter of Trout Unlimited Canada, which made numerous contributions to the publication of both editions of this book. I was generously allowed access to the research material they had gathered on the river. In addition, Trout Unlimited staff and former staff, including John Eisenhauer, Cheryl Bradley, Kerry Brewin, Dean Baayens and Don Pike, provided information and opinions, and read and corrected or verified portions of the manuscript.

The late Charles E. Brooks was the author of many angling books, including *The Living River*, a profile of Montana's Madison, which I unabashedly used as a model for this work. Charlie Brooks was one of my heroes, and it was a privilege of mine to show him the Bow River in 1979. After that he often helped and encouraged me with my writing in general and with the creation of this book in particular. Two other writers I am lucky to call friends also provided me with assistance. Russ Thornberry hired me as a guide on the Bow in 1976, giving me the opportunity to spend time on the river, and for many years Bob Scammell has provided encouragement and advice on the writing and book business. Thanks are also due Bob for the photographs that appear in the photo essay and on the cover of this book. Barry Mitchell also generously contributed photographs for the cover of the book.

Special thanks are due Jim Dixon, who first introduced me to the Bow and its trout in 1970, and to Al Sosiak and the late Bill Griffiths, who were biologists with the Fish and Wildlife Division of the Alberta government in the early 1980s. Their understanding of the Bow River extended beyond the scientific perspective to include the human. They provided me with technical information whenever I requested it, and their help was truly invaluable. Thanks must also be expressed to the other scientists, many anonymous, whose theses and reports I drew upon for pertinent technical information about the river.

I wish also to express thanks to Ernie Stenton, Mike Blenkarn, Bryan Kemper, Jim Branston, Jeff Gruttz, Martin Paetz, Shirley Charlton, Eric Grinnell, Neil Jennings, Don Cahoon, Rick Harding, Gary Borger, Dr. Erica Hargesheimer, Bruce Goodall, the city of Calgary, the Eastern Irrigation District and TransAlta Utilities.

When the decision was made in 1998 to revise and update this book, more help was required. Thanks first to Dennis Johnson and Johnson Gorman Publishers, who undertook this project. Glenn Smith is the fine flytier who graciously agreed to tie the flies that appear in Chapter 8. As well, thanks to Bob Vaile, Dan Bell, Dave Hughes, Ken Kohut, Bruce Morrison, Clive Schaupmeyer and Bill McMullen for valuable assistance.

Charles F. Waterman of DeLand, Florida, is one of North America's most respected outdoor writers. Though he and I spent just one day together on the Bow River many years ago, he has remained an inspiration and a generous advisor on the business of writing. Thanks, Charley, for the foreword to this book.

Lastly, special thanks must go to my wife, Lynda, and daughter, Deanna, who not only approve of this fly-fishing habit of mine but thankfully share my passion for it.

Introduction

THE BOW RIVER and I go back a long way—back to a time when, as songwriter Ian Tyson would put it, I was young and limber, and when the river was something of an upstart, too, breaking all the rules of trout riverdom. I note with pleasure that my affection for this river has not diminished in the 30 years since I first stepped into it; I note with less pleasure that the river seems to have aged more gracefully than I have.

A river's reputation, like a young athlete's or artist's, grows in a fairly predictable fashion: the first to notice their gifts are family members, then a few friends, then a writer from the local newspaper. Next is the national press, then an American TV network. Publicity reaches its zenith when yokels who knew them when they were nuttin' write books about them.

Things didn't work exactly this way for the Bow River—except for the book part. While I would never claim to have been the only guy around in the early days who appreciated the Bow and its trout fishing, in the mid-1970s the group of us was pretty small. If one of us saw somebody across the river with a fly rod, it wasn't hard to figure out who it was. Those of us fly-fishing the Bow then knew its trout were big and strong; we just didn't appreciate how much bigger and stronger they were than trout everywhere else.

In typical Canadian fashion it took high-profile outsiders—Lefty Kreh, A.J. McClane, Gary Borger—to point out that the fish in the Bow were bigger and stronger than the fish in the famous American rivers they had been writing about for many years. Ironically, among the last to find out about the quality of the Bow River was the average fly-fishing Albertan, who might have lived within sight of the Bow but continued dutifully plotting obligatory trips to the Madison, Snake and Henry's Fork. The last to meet and appreciate the charms of the Bow as a trout stream were the provincial government and the city of Calgary, both of which have made progress—albeit grudgingly at times—toward better stewardship of this resource.

The Bow has been pressured and abused by technology, pollution and simple accumulating humanity. But the river and its fish have survived, and just as importantly the river's appeal has survived. Solitude, the core element of fly-fishing, is still out there, even if it now must be sought more diligently. I still find it in the gold light of daybreak at McKinnon Flats or in the brittle, tangy aroma of an October afternoon.

The Bow's fish are as big and strong as ever, and though other rivers have taken their turn at being fashionable, it still draws anglers from far corners of the globe who return year after year. The great fishing brings them back, of course, but maybe they are drawn again and again to the Bow River because it is doing its best to disprove the saying that you can never go home. Often my visits to the river remind me not of what changes in life but of what remains constant. I hope they feel the same. The Bow isn't perfect, of course, any more than a spouse is perfect. But is a spouse worth spending a lifetime with? Unquestionably yes, and so is the Bow River.

The Whole
of the Bow

THE BOW RIVER rises in the Rocky Mountains of Banff National Park in southwestern Alberta and flows eastward 90 miles (144 km) to the city of Calgary. There it takes a southeastward direction through the prairie before finally joining the Oldman River at the Grand Forks, west of the city of Medicine Hat. The river drains an area of 9,800 square miles (25,382 km²) and travels 387 miles (623 km) from source to mouth, during which it flows through three distinct geographic zones: the mountains, the foothills and the prairie.

The stately prairie river that joins the Oldman gives little hint of the precocious white-water stream that kayakers covet in Banff National Park. Yet it is the same river, and a trip by air taking only a couple of hours would give a compressed view of the influences, both geological and human, that change its character.

Bow Lake, out of which the Bow River flows, is a cold, glacial

THE BOW RIVER BASIN

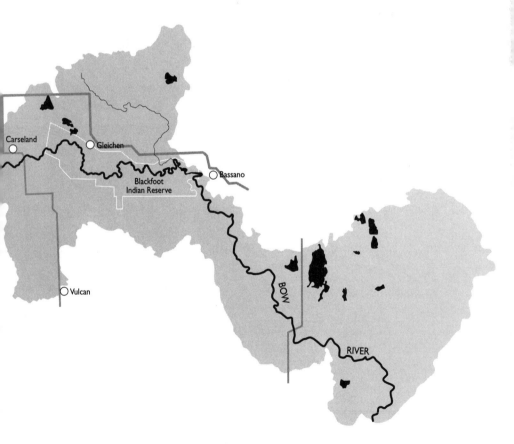

The Bow River in its upper reaches is very much a mountain stream.

lake located north of Lake Louise at an elevation of 6,353 feet (1,936 m). The lake is fed by Bow Glacier and several small trickles that drain off the mountains. The farthest upstream body of water identified on maps as the Bow River is one of these tiny feeders flowing into the lake through an alpine meadow to the north.

Downstream the river slides past Castle Mountain, which next to Lake Louise, is probably the most photographed spot in Banff National Park. Farther downstream yet, at the town of Banff, the river drops 32 feet (10 m) over Bow Falls and is joined by the Spray River. Though the river near Banff is a mountain stream, its character varies from the intimidating white-water stretches above Lake Louise to a braided section with numerous side channels near Canmore to a quiet, wide segment called Lac Des Arcs.

In the first part of its journey through Banff National Park the Bow River flows through what scientists call a subalpine ecoregion. The slopes facing southwest are warm and dry, and prevailing westerly breezes carry the fragrance of evergreens: Douglas fir, white spruce and lodgepole pine. In summer thousands of hikers and photographers stop to eat the wild strawberries and admire Indian paintbrush, mountain avens and fleabanes of various colors that grow along high-country trails.

In the autumn campers throughout the park are treated to a strange evening lullaby. Many of them probably don't realize what they are hearing, but the whistling bugle of the bull elk is the anthem of the high country. I enjoy it best filtered through the canvas walls of a tent, where I can visualize a great bull answering the challenge of another miles away on the other side of the valley. If the elk is the aristocrat of the park's deer family, surely the moose is the comical country cousin. In some abandoned channels along the Bow are lush willow bogs made to order for these homely giants.

In winter this region is combed by warm westerly Chinook winds that minimize the accumulation of snow and provide prime winter range for elk and bighorn sheep. These animals spend the winter at lower elevations, where they can be most easily admired by tourists.

It is the water near the town of Banff that receives the first attention from serious fly-fishers. Though long overlooked because of the fame of the river below Calgary, this part of the Bow has its own trouty charm. Between Banff and the Seebee dam, guides and anglers in McKenzie River driftboats float the river with their attention split between the beautiful trout water beneath them and the magnificent Rocky Mountains above. The scenery on an upper Bow float trip is rivaled in North America only by that on the Snake River of Wyoming.

From Bow Lake to its confluence with the Kananaskis River east of Canmore, the Bow is at the mercy of the Rockies. Glaciers flowed through this valley once, transforming it from a narrow, steep-walled gorge into what is today a surprisingly wide valley for a mountain river. The Bow flows through the Rockies clean, cold and fast, and carries a distinct aqua color in tribute to its glacial origins.

At Lac Des Arcs, downstream of the town of Canmore, the river swings from the southeast to the northeast, moving out of the mountains and into the foothills. In the upper foothills, vegetation is dominated by lodgepole pine, but when the river drops to an elevation of about 3,600 feet (1,097 m) near the Ghost dam, it cuts through aspen parkland, where areas of grassland are interspersed with mixed forest. It was here in one wide valley that I once counted a hundred white-tailed deer feeding in the brief, soft glow of a spring evening. Coyotes lurk around the edges of the fields, and bird watchers can find herons, geese, mergansers, ruffed grouse and a wide variety of birds of prey, from red-tailed and Swainson's hawks to bald eagles and great horned and great grey owls.

The river gets bigger and slower as it moves away from the mountains. At Calgary the Bow has a mean discharge of about 3,300 cubic feet (96 m^3) per second—about twice what it is at Banff—and an average width of 250–400 feet (76–122 m). The river's average gradient just above Calgary is about 18 feet per mile (3.4 m per km), a dramatic change of pace from those sections between Bow Lake and Lake Louise, where it drops nearly 80 feet per mile (15 m per km). Below Calgary the river is in much less of a hurry, with an average drop of about 5 feet per mile (1 m per km).

As the Bow flows through Calgary both people and nature dramatically alter the scenery along the river. The most obvious is the urban landscape of bridges, oil company towers, the Calgary Zoo and the Deerfoot Trail freeway that replaces the treed valley and windswept ridges of the upper river. Less immediately evident are the two contrasting geographic zones that collide at Calgary, but they can easily be seen on the drive south from the city on Highway 2. The rolling foothill ranch country is to the right, but a glance to the left shows the flat, treeless grainfields of the plains that stretch eastward over southern Alberta and Saskatchewan.

Downstream of Calgary the land on top is flat and dry, but the river valley is lush and green. The first time I saw this contrast was the first day I fished the river. Jim Dixon was showing it to me, and as we drove the straight, dusty gravel roads through wheat and barley fields, he expounded endlessly on the virtues of the magnificent trout stream we were about to fish. But something didn't seem right. This couldn't be trout country. Trout streams were supposed to be in mountains or foothills, or at least in places where trees grew. I wondered about this until we clanked across a cattle guard and drew to a dusty stop at the crest of a wide, green valley hidden from view until we were right on top of it.

The Bow River valley was like an oasis in a desert that day: cottonwood and spruce, willow and wildflowers on the valley floor and up the south side; prickly-pear cactus on the sandstone and clay banks of the north side; and a deep blue ribbon of water slicing through the middle of it all. Expensive horses and white-faced beef cattle shared the grass with mule deer. Red-tailed hawks and prairie falcons screamed at intruders from thermal currents high above.

Thirty years later a reprise of my first meeting with the Bow River occurs each time I crest the river breaks on the road to McKinnon Flats, a popular public access point on the Bow below Calgary. Thankfully little has changed. There is now a parking lot and boat ramp on the river, anglers and picnickers are busy on the shore and driftboats come and go. Bird life is especially diverse along the river today, and anglers can watch yellowlegs and sandpipers on the shore and cormorants and white pelicans above, the latter surely the most graceful of fliers. The shy great blue heron is here, too, stalking baitfish and small trout along the river's weedy edges. Huge greater Canada geese nest along the river in the spring, and on autumn evenings their honking fills the air as they flock up before leaving for the South. The view from the top is particularly stunning in the autumn, when gold wheat fields, blood-red willows and yellow cottonwoods are set off by the intense blue of the October sky. The river, too, seems bluer in the fall than at any other time of year.

The prairie above the river gets drier as the river works its way south and east, and though some adaptive species like mule deer and coyotes are found here, the wildlife is generally much different than in the foothills or mountains or even in the river valley itself. Coulees lined with buckbrush and willow run like veins through wheat, barley and canola fields above the lower Bow, and these are home to one native gamebird, the sharptail grouse, and two imports, the Hungarian partridge and the ring-necked pheasant. Farther east the windy, true shortgrass region between Brooks and Medicine Hat is home to antelope, sage grouse and rattlesnakes, which are occasionally found sunning themselves in the dry, rocky river breaks. Wildflowers are especially stunning on the prairie, probably because they stand out so strikingly against their drab surroundings. Early in spring, often while there is still snow on the ground, the prairie crocuses bloom, followed later by prickly roses, goldenrod and prairie sage.

After the Bow joins the Oldman River at the Grand Forks west of Medicine Hat, the new river is called the South Saskatchewan. Later it joins the North Saskatchewan River to become the Saskatchewan, which enters Lake Winnipeg in Manitoba. Bow River water eventually flows out of Lake Winnipeg in the Nelson River and ends its journey in Hudson Bay.

Through its journey the Bow River matures from a bold, laughing mountain stream to a prairie river of grace and dignity. Though some of its youth and innocence is lost along the way, the Bow today remains a treasure for its beauty, its abundance of wildlife and its gifts of recreation.

The recreational uses made of the Bow River system are as diverse as the landscape the river flows through. The upper portion flowing through Banff National Park is one of the most beautiful mountain settings in the world and attracts millions of visitors each year, from armchair explorers who view the mountains from a tour bus to experienced outdoor types who take advantage of the Bow Valley's world-class kayaking, canoeing, hiking, climbing, skiing, hunting and fishing.

The Bow River and its tributaries contain every class of water from expert to novice, making them a complete "paddling school." For seasoned veterans of the white-water set there is the Bow upstream of Lake Louise. Here the river often provides a cure for cockiness with a large dose of cold water. Many intermediate-level paddlers prefer the Bow between the Ghost dam and Cochrane, which contains some interesting riffles but is rated as Grade II water, where no ground scouting is required. This section is particularly popular early in the season because it is free of ice before most other waters. Excellent novice sections of water suitable for family day trips are found between Calgary and Carseland, with the most popular section probably being the run through Calgary from Bowness to Prince's Island.

The Bow's tributaries are popular with the canoe and kayak set, too. The upper Elbow has some of the best white water in western Canada, particularly on the stretch from Elbow Falls to Canyon Creek, which is known as a difficult piece of water with some Class VI rapids. It's a place for expert white-water paddlers only. Travel on the Elbow, however, is not allowed downstream of Twin bridges, 20 miles (32 km) west of Calgary. This land was formerly a military reserve and is reverting back to the Tsuu T'ina (formerly Sarcee) Indian Reserve.

The Kananaskis River, another tributary, has some Class III rapids and overall is considered a good intermediate white-water stream. A slalom course, built in the river downstream of the Barrier dam, is used by various clubs for racing and training. The Highwood River has a variety of water types, including some Class VI+ water below the provincial campsite on Highway 541, west of the town of Longview.

The varied character of the Bow River and its tributaries requires caution and good judgment on the part of all recreational users. Kayakers and canoeists are wise to be forewarned of the severe water-level fluctuation that occurs on the Bow between Canmore and the Bearspaw dam. They also must be aware of the location of dams and portages.

Those wishing to pursue kayaking or canoeing in the Bow system can obtain information and assistance from the numerous clubs in the Calgary area, including the Calgary Whitewater Club, the Calgary Canoe Club, the Bow Waters Canoe Club and others. A valuable introduction to paddling is found in Janice E. MacDonald's *Canoeing Alberta*, which provides information on the distances, degree of difficulty and access points on stretches of water in the Bow system. Travel Alberta provides accurate information on the flow of the Kananaskis River below Barrier dam, and Alberta Environmental Protection provides daily flow reports for most rivers on their Alberta River Report telephone line.

If dangling from a cliff is your idea of fun, you'll appreciate the other recreational opportunities available in the Bow corridor. Personally I have concluded that white-water paddlers are crazy but that mountain climbers are from another galaxy. Rock climbing is popular throughout the Rockies, particularly on the highly prized Mount Yamnuska in the front range of the Rockies near Canmore. Its pillars and chimney formations provide experienced climbers with some of the most challenging steep climbing in the world. A friend who partakes of the fishing below Calgary as well as the climbing and ski touring in the mountains told me that Mount Yamnuska is regarded by serious rock climbers the same way the Bow below Calgary is regarded by serious fly-fishers.

The upper Bow Valley corridor is perhaps best known throughout the world for its outstanding skiing. As well as downhill skiing at the resorts of Lake Louise, Sunshine Village, Mount Norquay and Nakiska, excellent cross-country skiing and ski touring are available throughout the valley.

Hunting, while not permitted in Banff National Park, is practiced in the Bow drainage outside the park boundaries. From the edge of the park east to the Stoney Indian Reserve, big game hunting is restricted to bow and arrow, as it is in the area immediately surrounding Calgary, including the Bow Valley as far east as the Highway 24 bridge. Along the lower portions of the Bow from Bassano to the Grand Forks, pheasant, sharptail grouse and Hungarian partridge hunters and their dogs share the draws and coulees with deer and antelope stalkers. The Bow Valley also offers excellent waterfowl shooting. Ducks are hunted extensively on the river downstream of Calgary, and geese are a prize highly sought by fanatics who spend all night digging pits and setting out decoys.

Fishing is a high-profile recreation throughout the Bow River system. Anglers have traditionally referred to the Bow above Calgary as the upper Bow and the river below the city as the lower Bow. For the sake of clarity, though, for the rest of this book I'll refer to the river from its headwaters to the Bearspaw dam as the upper Bow, the river from the Bearspaw through Calgary to the Bassano dam as the middle Bow and the river from Bassano to the Grand Forks as the lower Bow.

Several of the Bow's major tributaries join the river in the upper foothills region. None of these streams is especially productive, but most have decent populations of mountain whitefish, the occasional bull trout or native cutthroat, and varying numbers of rainbows. The Kananaskis River suffers from power-dam fluctuations although good fishing is available in both Upper and Lower Kananaskis lakes. The Ghost River, which joins the Bow about 10 miles (16.5 km) upstream of Cochrane, is relatively unproductive, lacking the nutrients necessary for algae growth. Jumpingpound Creek joins the Bow River from the south, upstream of Cochrane, and is regarded as a good trout stream. Access to its lower reaches is severely restricted by landowners, but upper sections are accessible.

Most of the Bow's tributaries also have beaver ponds, and a number have been stocked with rainbow or brook trout. Fish overwinter in some of these, and such ponds can provide good fishing for the still-water specialist.

Other opportunities for still-water fishing are found in the reservoirs above the dams in the foothills section of the river. Ghost Lake is a popular destination for the variety of fish it holds, including whitefish, and lake and rainbow trout. The reservoir is a real favorite of that peculiar breed of masochist called the ice fisherman, whose tents, snowmobiles, trucks and cars dot the reservoir throughout the winter. A friend of mine puts ice fishing right up there with moose hunting as a pursuit that, even when good, is still bad. He says he does it occasionally because it feels so good when he stops.

The Bearspaw reservoir has lake trout and rainbows, and produces good fishing for the latter when the fish cruise the flats on calm mornings and evenings. The river upstream of Bearspaw has good fishing on occasion for the trout that move up from the reservoir.

Overshadowing the upper Bow in most anglers' minds is the middle portion of the Bow system, which provides fine trout fishing in the mainstem Bow, its tributaries and reservoirs. The upper Elbow River is a clean, cold stream that carries nearly all of Alberta's cold-water sport fish, including bull trout. In the Glenmore reservoir, which was created by a dam on the Elbow in Calgary, anglers throw big spoons at the northern pike that predominate and occasionally haul out a big rainbow or brown trout as well. Fly-fishers take pike in the shallows along the edges of the reservoir in the Weaselhead area, where the Elbow enters the reservoir. The Elbow between the dam and its confluence with the Bow at Fort Calgary carries whitefish and brown trout, and could be an exceptional urban trout stream except for the instability that the dam causes.

The Highwood River is a major tributary joining the Bow from the south about halfway between Calgary and Carseland. It and most of its tributaries are primarily spawning and nursery streams for Bow River rainbow trout, and the fishing in these streams is usually (but not exclusively) for the small fish that have not yet moved down to the big river. The one exception is Cataract Creek, which joins the Highwood west of Longview. It has a resident population of rainbow and eastern brook trout, and is quite highly regarded by high-country anglers. Numbers of larger rainbows hold over in the lower reaches of the Highwood itself, and these fish are hunted by a few dedicated fly-fishers. The Highwood system also hosts an enormous run of mountain whitefish in the fall, when it is most heavily fished. The splendid ranchland through which the upper Highwood flows is some of the prettiest country in the province.

Starting some distance below Carseland, the Bow River begins to change from a cold-water to a warm-water fishery. Although trout have been taken by anglers as far as 8 miles (15 km) below the Bassano dam (well over 100 miles (161 km) downstream of Calgary), as the water slows and warms, the fishery gradually becomes dominated by warm-water species such as northern pike, walleye, goldeye and sauger.

Fish taken from the Bow below Bassano have been found to carry concentrations of mercury above safe levels for human consumption. Though the mercury is thought to occur in the fish because of its natural presence in the soil, the provincial government recommends that anglers not eat more than one meal per week of walleye or northern pike taken from this part of the river.

The Bow River is prized by many people for many reasons. To the young family with a canoe it is a pleasant Sunday afternoon outing. To the white-water folks it is a challenge and often a cold dunking. To the climbers it is fear and adrenaline. To the hunters it is the longed-for scent of October on the prairie. To the naturalists it is a classroom in which to observe myriad plant and animal species. To the historians it is a reference point for a large slice of Alberta's history.

When I close my eyes and think of the Bow River, many images crowd the stage. Rainbow trout sipping midsummer mayflies are quick to appear. So are the December mallards whistling downwind, my view of them blurred by frozen eyelashes. A hunter, who turns out to be me, stumbles down a coulee after a bird dog and then does nothing more strenuous than recline on the riverbank, looking up at a red-tailed hawk soaring against endless, billowy white clouds. Its flight takes me to a place where in imagination I can see a great, long way—in distance and in time. Time is the web in which history is trapped, and if I'm patient I can see both today's moments and history's eons, both the small vibrations and the huge sinewaves that define the rhythms of nature. Perhaps this sense of our place in the continuum of time is what the Bow River most deeply inscribes in those who visit it often.

2

A History
of the Bow
River Valley

THE BOW RIVER is very much a product of its journey
through time. But as with any history it is hard to decide
where to begin. Even the simple questions of when and how
the Bow River came into existence are difficult to answer con-
clusively because change is the constant in every river's life. Nevertheless it is generally agreed that the Bow has taken several different paths over the tens of thousands of years of its existence and has
emptied at different times into both the Hudson Bay, via its present
route, and the Gulf of Mexico, via the Missouri River system.

The Bow River is part of the legacy of the glaciers that covered much of prehistoric Alberta. Two major glaciers were active in
southern Alberta 55,000–40,000 years ago. The Laurentide Ice
Sheet, centered to the north and east, was moving southward, while
the Cordilleran Ice Sheet was crawling eastward out of the Rocky
Mountains. Tongues of the Cordilleran sheet flowed out of the
mountains through several valleys, but two major routes were the

Athabasca Valley, past the present-day towns of Jasper and Hinton, and the Bow Valley. The two glaciers met near what is today the intersection of Sarcee Trail and Richmond Road on the busy west edge of the city of Calgary. The spot is unceremoniously marked by a shopping center and pizza parlor. A better reminder of the power of ancient glacial action is the "Big Rock" located south of Calgary near the town of Okotoks. It is a glacial erratic, a quartzite rock the size of a large house that the glacier transported 200 miles (322 km) from Mount Edith Cavell in Jasper National Park.

When the climate of western North America began to warm, the smaller Bow Valley tongue of the Cordilleran Ice Sheet melted faster than the larger Laurentide. The meltwaters were deflected south by the Laurentide to gather in several large lakes, notably Glacial Lake Elbow and Glacial Lake Calgary, which had as its shorelines the crests of Nose Hill and Broadcast Hill in present-day Calgary. Meltwaters may have been forced far enough south to have become part of the Missouri–Mississippi drainage. Today, in deep southern Alberta, a ridge of land separates the Milk River (which flows into the Gulf of Mexico as part of the Missouri system) from the Oldman River (which flows into the Hudson Bay as part of the Saskatchewan system). As the Laurentide Glacier receded, the Bow River gradually shifted eastward in several stages until it found its current path 15,000–10,000 years ago.

NATIVE PEOPLES OF THE BOW

Though archaeological theories differ in their explanation of when and how the first occupants of the Bow Valley arrived, a common view is that when the climate warmed and the glaciers slowly receded, prehistoric people made their way about 11,500 years ago across a land bridge in the Bering Strait between Siberia and Alaska, and then trekked down a narrow, ice-free north–south corridor through west central Alberta. A rival theory gaining currency among scientists holds that the first inhabitants of the Americas migrated down the West Coast in skin-covered boats as early as 30,000 years ago and then made their way north as the glaciers

Blackfoot Indian encampment near Fort Macleod, 1902.

receded. From whatever direction they arrived, prehistoric people likely settled in the Calgary area for reasons that still exist: there were few topographic barriers to north–south travel, the Bow River valley provided a logical route to the mountains as well as a good source of wood for shelter and fire, and the winters were moderated by the warm Chinook winds. To the east the grasslands carried endless herds of buffalo, which became the mainstay of Plains Indian culture.

When whites arrived in the late eighteenth century, the Bow Valley was the domain of the Blackfoot Nation, a group of Plains Indians made up of three tribes: the Blood, the Peigan and the Blackfoot proper (presumably so named because the soles of their moccasins were blackened from the ash of prairie grassfires).

The Blackfoot lived a nomadic, communal lifestyle that depended upon the buffalo. They wore clothing and lived in shelters made from buffalo hides, they ate pemmican made from buffalo meat and they fashioned implements from buffalo bones. When the buffalo were abundant everyone shared the wealth; when the buffalo were elusive everyone shared the hunger. The Blackfoot had great respect for this creature and considered it a holy animal, a gift from the sun.

The Blackfoot pursued the buffalo herds through most of southern Alberta, ambushing them with bow and arrow or stampeding them over steep embankments. One such buffalo jump was located on the Bow River above its confluence with the Highwood, and buffalo bones may still be found there today. Other buffalo jumps were scattered about southern Alberta. Today they are designated provincial historical sites and bear colorful names such as Head-Smashed-In Buffalo Jump and Old Women's Buffalo Jump.

In the seventeenth century the Beaver Indians, a woodland tribe from northern Alberta, drifted south into the area occupied by the Blackfoot. They came to be called the Sarcee. Although unrelated to the Blackfoot they became culturally integrated and adopted much of the Blackfoot lifestyle.

About 1730 the Blackfoot acquired horses from other Indian tribes to the south and west. Around the same time they obtained guns from the Cree, who had acquired them from French and English fur traders. The combination of horse, gun and abundant buffalo allowed the Blackfoot to thrive as a culture and dominate life on the Alberta plains for much of the remainder of the eighteenth century.

Arriving after the Blackfoot were the Stoney, who occupied the region just east of the Rockies at the time of the white man's arrival. The Stoney were the westernmost group of the Assiniboine and had migrated across the prairies from their original home near the western edge of the Great Lakes. The Stoney were of great value to white explorers because they were capable guides who were familiar with the mountain passes.

THE ARRIVAL OF EUROPEANS

Different groups of people with different purposes helped open up the Bow River valley to Canadian settlement and development. They were, in short, the explorers who searched for a route through the Rocky Mountains, the fur traders who came to satisfy Europe's insatiable appetite for beaver pelts, the missionaries who came to convert the aboriginal peoples to Christianity, the law enforcers who came to bring order to the lawless frontier, the railway builders who knit the new nation of Canada together, and the ranchers and oilmen who saw opportunity in southern Alberta's abundant resources.

When seventeen-year-old David Thompson, who later became a famous fur trader and geographer of the Canadian West, wintered in southern Alberta in 1787, he journeyed to the junction of two beautiful, clear rivers—the Swift, which later came to be called the Elbow, and the river the Peigan knew as the *Manachaban,* meaning "the river where bow reeds grow." Their name referred to the tree from which they made their bows, a tree later to be named the Douglas fir. The river was appropriately known to early explorers as the Cold Water River. But David Thompson named it the Bow River, and this name first appeared on a map produced in 1801 by the English cartographer Arrowsmith.

The major fur trading center in southern Alberta in the early nineteenth century was the Hudson's Bay Company post located at Rocky Mountain House, 90 miles (145 km) north of the Bow at the junction of the Clearwater and North Saskatchewan rivers. In 1832 the operation was terminated, and a replacement was constructed by the Hudson's Bay Company on the banks of the Bow. Called Peigan Post, it was located west of present-day Morley at the Bow's confluence with Bow Fort Creek. Peigan Post was likely the first attempt at white settlement on the Bow River, but it was a short-lived effort, and after just two years of operation the fort was closed.

Closely following the explorers and traders into southern Alberta were missionaries of many denominations. Facing physical hardship in a new land but fueled by the fire of their conviction, they sowed the first seeds of Christianity in Alberta. The first to see the Bow Valley was the English Wesleyan Reverend Robert Rundle. He traveled up the Bow and camped on the Spray River in June 1841 near the mountain later named in his honor. Rundle was an effective missionary, greatly respected by the Indians, with whom

he lived from 1840–1848. In 1873 the Methodist missionary George
McDougall, who had earlier opened a church at Edmonton, arrived
with his son, John, and established a successful mission and ranch
near Morley.

    The Roman Catholic Church also sent missionaries to British
North America, including Father Pierre Jean de Smet, who came
from Oregon to Alberta, and Father Leon Joseph Doucet, who
worked with the Blackfoot near Calgary. Father Doucet was the
first priest in charge of the chapel built at Fort Calgary in 1877.

    From 1864–1874 Alberta was characterized by chaos and law-
lessness. The American Fur Company went bankrupt in 1864, and
American free traders, along with soldiers discharged at the end of
the Civil War, flooded into Alberta. Many of them took to trading
with the Blackfoot, obtaining furs and buffalo hides in exchange for
whiskey of dubious origin that often contained, among other
things, chewing tobacco, Jamaica ginger, red peppers, tea leaves,
molasses and even red ink. W.F. Butler, a government official sent to
investigate, reported that it was a region "without law, order, or

George
McDougall
monument,
Pakan,
Alberta,
1956.

Fort Whoop-Up, the largest of several American free-trader posts in southern Alberta.

security for life or property; robbery and murder for years have gone unpunished; Indian massacres are unchecked; and all civil and legal institutions are entirely unknown."

The bold and defiant whiskey traders even set up trading posts to compete with the legal traders from the Hudson's Bay Company, which operated out of Fort Edmonton to the north. They often gave their illicit businesses outrageous, colorful names. The most notorious of these were Fort Whoop-Up (the major whiskey post), Standoff and Slide-Out. Whiskey, coupled with the slaughter of the buffalo and white diseases such as smallpox, had a devastating effect on aboriginal peoples. Those left were completely poverty stricken by 1874.

That same year a contingent of the newly formed North-West Mounted Police (whose name was changed in 1920 to Royal Canadian Mounted Police) was sent west to rid the region of the American whiskey traders and to restore law and order on the Alberta plains. Led by skilled guide Jerry Potts, the rookie police force made its way to deep southern Alberta and to a river Potts called de Ole Man's River. The Mounties built a fort on an island in the Oldman

LEFT: The legendary Mounted Police scout Jerry Potts, 1877.

RIGHT: Colonel James F. Macleod of the North-West Mounted Police.

A contingent of North-West Mounted Police sent west to bring law to the Alberta frontier.

River and named it Fort Macleod after one of their commanders, Colonel James F. Macleod.

Colonel Macleod was a worthy leader, quickly proving himself to the Blackfoot people with his effective actions against the whiskey traders. Crowfoot, the Blackfoot chief, was skeptical about

Fort Calgary was established at the confluence of the Bow and Elbow rivers.

the coming of the police, but he also recognized what damage was being done to his people by the whiskey trade. Crowfoot was a perceptive and intelligent man who came to respect the efforts of Colonel Macleod and his redcoats. Over time the two men developed a lasting admiration for each other.

In 1875 "F" Troop of the North-West Mounted Police, commanded by Inspector E.A. Brisebois, was sent north from Fort Macleod to establish a new fort at the confluence of the Bow and Elbow rivers. Brisebois reasoned that the new fort should be named after him, but he was overruled by Colonel Macleod, who suggested the name *Calgary*, which means "clear running water" in Gaelic and which was the name of a castle belonging to members of his mother's family on the Island of Mull.

The contract for constructing the fort was given the I.G. Baker Company out of Fort Benton, Montana. When the fort was completed, the company established a trading post, and a village quickly sprang up around it.

In 1877 the Blackfoot agreed to give up their land to the Cana-

*"Halt!"—
an early
painting
celebrating
the arrival
of law and
order on the
frontier.*

*The I.G.
Baker
trading post
was one of
the first
commercial
enterprises
in Calgary.*

Fort Macleod 10 years after the arrival of the North-West Mounted Police.

dian government in return for a small sum of money, some cattle and agricultural tools. They relinquished about 50,000 square miles (130,000 km²) of territory that encompassed part of southern Saskatchewan and all of Alberta from the Red Deer River south to the 49th parallel. The Indians would be free to hunt on their ancestral lands as long as the buffalo lasted, after which they were to move to reserves of their choosing. This historic agreement, Treaty No. 7, was signed by Crowfoot and other leaders of the Blackfoot Confederacy in September 22, 1877, at Blackfoot Crossing on the Bow River near the present-day town of Cluny.

With the buffalo hunted to near-extinction the Blackfoot could not continue their nomadic tradition, and their condition quickly deteriorated. Starvation compounded by disease left them little choice but to move to the reserves allotted them in Treaty No. 7. Attempts were made to transform them into farmers, but their spirit had been broken by the disappearance of the buffalo and the loss of their lands, and they could not adapt to the white man's sedentary agricultural lifestyle.

Some traders turned to legitimate business after the Mounties put an end to the whiskey trade. The colorful Harry "Kamoose" Taylor established the Macleod Hotel that boasted the sale of "every known fluid except water."

Thus the Blackfoot were passed by in what was quickly becoming a swift rush toward European immigration. The once numerous Sarcee were similarly decimated by starvation and disease. By 1877 just 255 Sarcee were left alive. Today they are called Tsuu T'ina, and their reserve sits at the southwest edge of the city of Calgary. The Stoney were more fortunate than the Plains Indians, for they lived in a more diverse mountain and foothill environment and so were not as dependent on the buffalo for survival. Nevertheless their culture declined as well, worn down by the continued imposition of white European culture.

An era ended on April 25, 1890, when the courageous and peace-loving Crowfoot died at Blackfoot Crossing. He was buried overlooking his Bow River and the crocus-dotted plains that for most of his life had supported mighty herds of buffalo and a proud nation of Blackfoot people. His last days could not have been happy as he reflected on the changes wrought upon his land and his people by the coming of the white man. Today, on a grassy hillside above the Bow River, a simple plaque marks the spot where he

*Chief
Crowfoot.
He made
his word
and he kept
his word.*

erected his tepee for the last time. During Treaty No. 7 negotiations,
Crowfoot had made the famous pronouncement that contained the
kernel of his wisdom:

> *Our land is more valuable than your money. It will last forever. It
> will not perish as long as the sun shines and the water flows, and
> through all the years it will give life to men and beasts. It was put
> there by the great spirit and we cannot sell it because it does not
> belong to us.*

Many years would pass before anything reminiscent of Crowfoot's ethic would find expression again in the Bow River watershed. In the meantime there would be settlement and development that would change the character of the Bow River forever.

THE RAILWAY

In 1880 the Bow River valley was chosen as the westward route for the Canadian Pacific Railway. The CPR had been an idea for several years, and in fact as early as 1859 an expedition had been mounted by Captain John Palliser to search for a possible route through the Rocky Mountains. Nothing further was accomplished, however, until the province of British Columbia threatened to secede from Canadian confederation unless construction was started.

Once construction was underway, progress on the railroad was surprisingly quick, and the first train pulled into Calgary amid much fanfare and excitement in August 1883. The workers had laid 180 miles (290 km) of track from Medicine Hat to Calgary in just two months.

From Calgary the railroad pushed westward into increasingly rugged country, up the Bow Valley past Mount Rundle and Cascade Mountain and over the route taken by George Simpson, an early explorer in the Bow region. After clawing its way over the Kicking Horse Pass into the Selkirk Mountains of interior British Columbia, the historic last spike was driven on November 7, 1885, at Craigellachie and the railroad was complete.

With this remarkable achievement Canada was truly linked together from Atlantic to Pacific, and Fort Calgary, on the banks of the Bow River, ceased to be simply a stop on the trail north from Fort Macleod to Edmonton. Settlers now had easy access to inviting land, and forestry, grain farming and ranching became viable industries because the Canadian Pacific Railway made possible the flow of products and supplies throughout southern Alberta. The coming of the railroad made Calgary the focal point of this increased activity, and what had been a simple North-West Mounted Police fort in 1875 was a thriving city within a decade.

The Canadian Pacific Railway built its depot near the banks of the Elbow River, west of Fort Calgary.

The railway also encouraged settlement elsewhere, and in 1883 a section house and log station were built at railway Siding 29 near the confluence of the Bow and Spray rivers. Lord Strathcona would later name it Banff in honor of Banffshire, Scotland, the birthplace of two CPR railway officials.

BANFF

In 1885 William Pearce, Superintendent of Mines, visited the hot springs at Banff and urged the federal government to set aside the area as a park. Pearce argued that a European-style spa near the hot springs would attract tourists to the area and would be profitable for the Canadian government. On November 25, 1885, an Order in Council was passed by the federal parliament to establish Banff Hot Springs Reserve. In 1887 the name was changed to Rocky Mountains Park Reserve.

By this time 650 permanent residents resided in the park, and the celebrated Banff Springs Hotel opened its doors for business on

With the coming of the railroad Calgary was rapidly transformed into an important trading center for southern Alberta.

The railway station at Canmore, just outside the boundary of the national park, 1912.

Banff, c. 1883. The coming of the railway would transform the mountain wilderness into a bustling tourist center.

Anglers on the river, c. 1900.

The Cave and Basin Hot Springs immediately attracted visitors to the Rockies with its European-style spa.

The Canadian Pacific Railway was quick to capitalize on the tourist potential of the national park by constructing its famed Banff Springs Hotel above Bow Falls.

June 1, 1888. That year 5,000 tourists traveled by rail to enjoy the waters of the Cave and Basin Hot Springs, delighting the federal government and making Superintendent Pearce look very good in the process.

The size of the park grew over the next 40 years as additional tracts of land were added. In 1930 the National Parks Act was passed, making all federal parks national parks of Canada. At the same time the name Rocky Mountains Park was changed to Banff National Park. The act stated that "National Parks are dedicated to the Canadian people for their benefit, education and enjoyment, but they must be left unimpaired for the pleasure of future generations." Today Banff National Park encompasses 2,600 square miles (6,734 km²) of some of the finest mountain scenery in the world and attracts over six million visitors annually.

RANCHING

An abundance of water and grazing land, the shelter of river valleys and coulees, and the moderating effect of Chinook winds in winter made the foothills east of the Rockies ideal cattle territory, and the new railroad gave the ranchers a means of moving their cattle to market. Southern Alberta quickly became prime beef country.

One of the early prominent ranchers in the area was Senator M.H. Cochrane, a cattle breeder from Quebec, who began working 100,000 acres (40,470 ha) on the Bow River west of Calgary in 1881. The Cochrane Ranch supplied beef to the North-West Mounted Police for several years before the operation was moved south to a location near the Montana border.

Perhaps Alberta's best-known pioneer rancher was John Ware, an Afro-American who had been born a slave in South Carolina. Ware arrived in the Highwood area of southern Alberta in 1882 and built a ranch on the headwaters of the Sheep River. His ranch was not large, but this didn't prevent John Ware from becoming one of early Alberta's most respected citizens, known throughout the province for his integrity and ranching skill. Ware Creek, a tribu-

(B297.) RANCHING SCENE IN ALBERTA. SHEEP. 1883.

tary to the Sheep River and an important spawning stream for Bow River trout, is named in his honor.

Sheep grazing on the Cochrane Ranch, 1883.

Another engaging character in the early Alberta ranching industry was, strangely enough, Edward, Prince of Wales, who would later abdicate the British throne to marry divorcée Wallace Simpson. The prince visited Alberta in 1919, fell in love with the landscape and purchased a ranch on Pekisko Creek, 65 miles (105 km) southwest of Calgary. On the occasion of the Prince's first meeting with prominent Alberta cattlemen, the rancher who drew the tricky task of introducing the parties got past the awkwardness by stating simply, "Boys, this is the prince. He's a hell of a good fellow!"

The Prince's occasional visits to his ranch no doubt created quite a stir among early Calgarians, but the real excitement was happening just a few miles away from his ranch at Turner Valley, where the economic future of the young province was being forged.

*Alberta's
"Big Four"
pioneer
ranchers—
(L–R)
Patrick
Burns,
George
Lane,
Archie
McLean
and Alfred
Cross—
pose with
the Duke
of Windsor
(center).*

OIL

The energy industry that was to become the pillar of Alberta's economy also had its beginnings early in the twentieth century. As early as 1903 some natural gas wells were producing for the city of Calgary, but it was in 1914, when oil was struck near Turner Valley, southwest of Calgary, that the prospect of a black gold bonanza sent the city oil crazy. Dozens of exploration companies were launched, and shares traded at exorbitant prices. The fuss subsided, however, with the outbreak of the World War I later that same year. After the war more oil was discovered, and the industry took up where it had left off. The Turner Valley oilfield, the first such oilfield in the British Empire, was turning Alberta into a boom province by 1936. Over the next five years 200 wells were drilled in the area, and remarkably only six turned up dry. By 1942 Turner Valley was producing 10 million barrels of oil per year.

Since then, through cycles of boom and bust, the oil industry has been the engine driving Calgary's growth from a frontier out-post into a modern metropolitan center. Calgary's growth would shape the future of the Bow River, for growing populations require water—lots of water—for power, for irrigation, for municipal and industrial purposes, and every drop must come from the Bow River and its tributaries.

DAMS AND DIVERSIONS

For most of the twentieth century people have been making efforts to transform the Bow River into something better suited to their needs. The result has been a surprisingly large number of dams, diversions, weirs, reservoirs and alterations to the flow of the Bow River and its tributaries.

In the 1920s the growing city of Calgary needed a permanent water supply, so in 1929 construction began on the Glenmore dam on the Elbow River about 7 miles (11 km) above its confluence with the Bow. Completed in 1932 the Glenmore reservoir was the sole source of Calgary's municipal water until 1973, when it began sharing the job with the Bearspaw plant. The Glenmore reservoir is attractive, surrounded by parks and bicycle paths that make it a pop-ular urban recreation area. Sailing and fishing (chiefly for pike) are popular on the reservoir.

The Glenmore and Bearspaw dams provide water to the city, but the rest of the developments are for one of two things: power or irrigation. Upstream of Calgary the river and its tributaries are used to produce electricity, and downstream the water is used for irrigation.

POWER PRODUCERS

Industrial growth in the early twentieth century brought demands for sources of electrical power in Alberta, and the first hydroelectric dam was constructed on the Bow by Calgary Power (now TransAlta Utilities) at Horseshoe Falls, west of Morley, in 1911. This development supplied electricity to Calgary via the first

Early
recreation
on the
Glenmore
reservoir.

long-distance transmission line in the province and spurred growth in the young manufacturing industry in Calgary.

Two years later a dam was built on the Bow immediately below its confluence with the Kananaskis River, near the town of Seebee, and in 1930 the largest man-made reservoir on the Bow was created with the construction of the Ghost dam. Located just below the confluence of the Ghost and Bow rivers, the dam and hydro plant delivered power to the city of Edmonton, 180 miles (290 km) north.

In addition to the power developments on the Bow itself, numerous diversions and dams have been constructed on its tributaries. Lake Minnewanka, northeast of Banff, was strategically located to allow the diversion of water from two rivers into the lake. In 1941 the Cascade River was diverted into the west end of the lake, raising its level by 65 feet (20 m) and increasing its area by 35 percent. The upper Ghost River, conveniently flowing past the east end of Lake Minnewanka, also was channeled into the lake. Water stored in Minnewanka is used to produce power at the Cascade hydro plant.

The Kananaskis River, a tributary joining the Bow from the south, has three dams and hydro plants interrupting its flow: Interlakes (situated between Upper and Lower Kananaskis Lakes), Pocaterra (located at the outlet of the lower lake) and Barrier (located several miles above the river's confluence with the Bow).

In 1951 a dam was built on the Spray River at the outlet of Spray Lake, southeast of Banff, which enlarged the lake and created the Spray Lakes reservoir. Water channeled out the north end of the reservoir through a series of canals and penstocks drops 1,200 feet (366 m) in 7 miles (11 km) between the reservoir and the Bow River. Along the way it drives three hydro plants.

All told, the Bow has been tampered with plenty in the twentieth century. The score-card reads 11 major dams or diversions and 11 hydro plants in the upper Bow system. Total power production from the Bow and its tributaries is 327 megawatts.

It is not clear exactly what effect the dams and reservoirs have had on the Bow as a fishery. The first study of possible repercussions of power development on fish populations in the Bow system was not completed until 1947, but because no biological data existed prior to hydroelectric development, no comparisons could be made. The writer of that report, D.S. Rawson of the University of Saskatchewan, did suggest that the dams existent at that time had relatively little impact on the fishery. He reasoned that the upper Bow River had presumably been only moderately productive before power development because of the considerable fluctuation in water volume from natural causes. Today others argue that the short-term fluctuations caused by hydro plants, including those major projects completed since Rawson's report, are more detrimental to the fishery than the natural fluctuations that existed prior to power development.

Rawson nevertheless was of the opinion that subsequent developments on the Kananaskis River would severely damage that stream as a fishery. He was correct. The Kananaskis today is a poor trout stream as a result of frequent, severe fluctuations in water level caused by dams. For example, in 1979 the Kananaskis below Barrier dam had its highest daily discharge on May 19 at 1,015 cubic feet

(30 m^3) per second and its lowest daily discharge just four days later at 5 cubic feet (.15 m^3) per second.

It is generally agreed that the reservoirs above Calgary have reduced the likelihood of damaging floods of the sort that occurred between 1897 and 1932. The most severe of five major floods, in 1897, was estimated to have produced a discharge of 99,000 cubic feet (2,885 m^3) per second in the city of Calgary, a staggering 30 times the river's mean discharge and 10 times its volume during heavy spring runoff. The reservoirs are filled over the course of the spring and summer so that water will be available to handle the increased demands for power in the winter months. Consequently spring water levels in the river today are lower than would naturally occur.

The Bow, like most northern rivers, is subject to wintertime formation of icejams in river channels. At their most extreme, icejams may block the incoming flow and flooding may occur. As early as 1896 this was a problem for Calgary, and it became more serious as the city grew and more buildings were erected near the river. In an attempt to reduce the problem of icejams and flooding in Calgary, the Bearspaw dam was completed in 1954 to regulate the flow of the Bow River downstream through Calgary. While opinions varied about its potential success prior to its construction, the flooding problem has been reduced significantly since the dam's completion. Today, in addition to regulating flow, the Bearspaw dam also produces electrical power and a significant portion of Calgary's municipal water.

The bad news regarding dams and reservoirs in the Bow system is that those upstream of the Bearspaw are responsible for extremely severe short-term (day-to-day or even hour-to-hour) water level fluctuations that limit the river's productivity as a fishery and create problems for the Bow River's recreational users. The good news is that the Bearspaw dam reduces the likelihood of springtime flooding and decreases damaging fluctuations in water level created by the other power projects upstream. The great news is that trout in the Bow River through and below Calgary were an unintentional beneficiary of efforts to stabilize the river.

BASSANO DAM
JULY 4, 1924

IRRIGATION

The eastern half of southern Alberta is dry grassland, and much effort has been expended to spread the water from the South Saskatchewan River system around for agricultural use. As a result irrigation is the single largest user of water in the Bow River system. As early as 1908 a diversion weir was constructed in Calgary below Prince's Island to divert a portion of the Bow's water to the Western Irrigation District, a block of agricultural land east of Calgary and north of the river. In 1918, near the town of Carseland, 40 miles (64 km) downstream of Calgary, another diversion weir was constructed. Here water from the Bow was diverted south and channeled through Lake McGregor and Travers reservoir to supply water to the Bow River Irrigation District in the deep south of the province.

Farther downstream at the town of Bassano a major dam and reservoir were completed in 1914. Built by the Canadian Pacific

The Bassano dam 10 years after construction. The huge structure feeds over 1,000 miles (1,640 km) of irrigation canals in southern Alberta.

Railway the project was designed to provide water to an area that in 1935 came to be called the Eastern Irrigation District, an enormous tract of land between the Bow and Red Deer rivers. The Bassano dam is an impressive structure (if one is impressed by these kinds of things). It consists of an earthen embankment 45 feet (14 m) high and 7,200 feet (2,195 m) long and a concrete spillway 720 feet (220 m) long and 40 feet (12 m) high across the river's channel. When filled, the Bassano reservoir occupies 988 acres (400 ha). The dam annually diverts 500,000 acre feet (61,674 ha m) of Bow River water into 1,186 miles (1,909 km) of irrigation canals.

The engineers who planned the Bassano dam were unknowingly developing a tourist attraction for this part of southern Alberta. The overgrown irrigation ditches and adjacent fields of grain combined to provide marvelous habitat for ring-necked pheasants, which in turn attracted pheasant hunters. The town of Brooks has for years been known as the pheasant capital of Canada.

Water from the Highwood River has been diverted for irrigation since 1905. At Squaw Coulee, west of the town of High River, water is channeled south into Mosquito Creek. A second diversion at High River channels water into the Little Bow River to irrigate land south and east of Calgary.

If David Thompson, Chief Crowfoot or Colonel Macleod were to tour the Bow Valley today, they might find the view familiar in the protected area through Banff National Park or in the largely undeveloped shortgrass prairie in the deep south near Gleichen. But if they saw the city of Calgary and the dams and reservoirs on the middle section of the river, they might wonder how their "river where the bow reeds grow" could have produced all this. For the Bow River and many of its tributaries are now anything but free-flowing rivers. The impact humans have had on the river and valley is great, but it is a tribute to the durability of such things as rivers that they refuse to be completely tamed and placed under the thumb of progress.

CHAPTER

3

A History
of the Bow
River Trout
Fishery

THE BOW RIVER downstream of Calgary has been acclaimed as one of the best trout streams in the world. Yet this high-quality fishery, which has been attracting attention from the international angling community for over 25 years, is in essence a fluke because the river has been the unintentional beneficiary of numerous man-made alterations. None of these changes was made with the intent of improving the river as a trout stream, but improve it they did, and the fishery today exists as if it had been very carefully planned. It has been called "a magnificent accident" by one outdoor writer who visited it. Another termed it "the most misunderstood fishery in North America." Both were correct.

Over 10,000 years ago, after the glaciers receded and the Bow River established its present course, the upper portion of the river was inhabited by cutthroat trout, bull trout (formerly called Dolly Varden) and mountain whitefish. These native species are thought

55

Anglers with a large bull trout captured in the upper Bow in the autumn of 1945.

to have found their way into the Bow via lakes on the continental divide in British Columbia that simultaneously drained east and west. The native fish of the lower portion of the Bow are northern pike, walleye, goldeye and white suckers, all of which are thought to have moved into the Bow from the Missouri system when the two drainages were connected in early post-glacial times.

The earliest angling reports from around 1900 suggest that upper Bow cutthroat trout (then called speckled or mountain trout) occasionally attained a weight of 6–7 pounds (2.7–3.2 kg) and that they "rose well to the fly." The bull trout were reported to reach weights of 12–14 pounds (5.5–6.4 kg) but were less readily caught with flies.

Alberta's native fish were no doubt appreciated by early settlers, but it wasn't long before they began stocking fish, partly because they'd begun to notice the decline in the native stocks that their angling had caused and partly because human beings possess an innate desire to tamper with wildlife in the name of sport. The reverence for native species prevalent today was not part of pioneer mentality.

Most early efforts at stocking fish in the Bow and its tributaries were concentrated in the Banff area, but records are sketchy, and it appears that a substantial number of early attempts were not recorded at all. Eastern brook and rainbow trout, occasionally reported in anglers' catches as early as 1900, were apparently planted in the Bow, but the exact dates of the introductions are not known for either species. It is believed that employees of the Canadian Pacific Railway undertook a considerable amount of unscientific fisheries management by moving fish from one body of water to another. Perhaps the most peculiar early fish planting was the unsuccessful attempt in 1901–02 to introduce smallmouth bass into Lake Minnewanka.

Our present-day alarm with the diminishing quality of sport fishing is not a new phenomenon. In 1890 J.H. McIllree of the North-West Mounted Police prepared a report on the status of stream fishing in the Calgary area in which he expressed concern over the depletion of fish populations caused by netting and trapping when the fish were running up the tributaries to spawn. He concluded that the streams needed more protective regulations— closed seasons, minimum sizes and a ban on the dumping of sawdust into the river by sawmills—and he encouraged stocking of the streams.

Twenty years later circumstances had become worse. A sitting

The beautiful Lake Minnewanka, c. 1885, which was the scene of an ill-fated attempt to introduce smallmouth bass into the Canadian Rockies.

of the Alberta and Saskatchewan Fisheries Commission in 1910 concluded that "Our streams are all depleted and one or two fish are now taken where a basketful could be caught ten years ago." Other complaints suggested that railway construction, coal washing and sawmill pollution were damaging the fisheries.

Two attempts were made to resolve the problem of a shrinking fishery. First, in 1913 a fish hatchery was constructed at Banff just upstream of Bow Falls on the south side of the Bow River. Second, in 1915 the first fishing season was established in Rocky Mountain Park (now Banff National Park). A fishing license was required, and the limit was set at 15 fish per day with a minimum size of 7 inches (18 cm).

Stocking records are more complete thereafter, and they indicate that cutthroat trout imported from the United States were planted in Banff park waters in 1915. The cutthroat also was the principal fish stocked in the Bow and its tributaries between 1929 and 1938. Native cutthroats from the Spray Lakes were introduced initially. Later Washington State coastal cutthroats and Yellowstone

cutthroats reared at a hatchery in Cranbrook, British Columbia, were stocked in the Bow.

Fish hatchery at Calgary, 1940.

The province's stocking policy changed in 1939, and from then until 1947 rainbow trout were the favored and most commonly stocked fish in the Bow system, largely because they were available, easy to raise in hatcheries and possessed sporting qualities appreciated by anglers.

The first of the Bow River fishery's genuinely fortunate accidents occurred when brown trout were introduced into the river. The Scottish strain of brown trout called the Loch Leven had been brought to the hatchery at Banff in 1924. In 1925 a truck carrying brown trout destined for more distant Alberta streams had a breakdown at the Carrot Creek bridge upstream of Canmore. Rather than let the fish die the driver released the 45,000 fry into the creek. This one accidental stocking has resulted in the successful proliferation of brown trout in the Bow from Banff to well below Calgary.

In Alberta in the late 1940s the practice of stocking hatchery fish in streams capable of natural propagation was studied by Dr. R.B. Miller. His investigation concluded that hatchery fish suffered heavy mortality when planted in streams and that very few lived to spawn. As a result the routine stocking of yearling and fingerling trout in Alberta streams was virtually abandoned in 1952. So the rainbows and browns in the middle Bow today, while not native, are most certainly wild, having been hatched and reared in the river and its tributaries.

In this regard fisheries management in Alberta was ahead of most other jurisdictions. Seventeen years after the province abandoned the practice of stocking hatchery catchables, the State of Montana conducted a study into the effectiveness of stocking fish 7 inches (18 cm) and longer in the Madison River and reached the same verdict. Some of the findings in this study were very surprising. Charles Brooks relates in his marvelous book about the Madison, *The Living River,* that when the stocking of hatchery catchables was terminated, the number of wild fish 7 inches (18 cm) and longer *quadrupled* in a single year. Montana consequently stopped stocking hatchery catchables in its best trout streams in 1972. The practice has since become widely accepted in the field of wild trout stream management.

In 1942 the Bow downstream of Calgary was said to carry more trout per mile than any other stream in Canada. Oddly this report appeared in a pollution survey of the river. The same survey reported that water quality was not only poor but that it constituted a potential health hazard because of high coliform bacteria counts. Both facts could be attributed to the city's municipal sewage, which was receiving only primary treatment before entering the river. The Bow's large trout population was partly the result of this effluent-enriched water that supported prolific plant and insect communities.

Also contributing to the middle Bow's substantial fish population was the Bearspaw dam. Before its construction winter flows through Calgary dropped to as low as 305 cubic feet (9 m^3) per second, which allowed concentrations of nutrients from municipal sewage to increase to dangerous levels. After the dam was completed in 1954, winter flows were maintained near 1,800 cubic feet (52 m^3) per second, which kept the nutrients adequately diluted and maintained sufficient dissolved oxygen for fish to overwinter.

These, then, were the two artificial factors that aided the development of the trout fishery below Calgary. The nutrients from the city's effluent stimulated plant, insect and trout growth, and the Bearspaw dam stabilized the formerly erratic flow levels. It is important to note, however, that these factors alone did not create the fishery. It was the combination of these factors plus some crucial natural characteristics of the river—namely suitable water temperature and trout habitat, and proximity to good spawning grounds—that created the blue ribbon fishery on the Bow River below Calgary.

Human activity initially helped produce an extraordinary trout stream, but continued activity thereafter has threatened the river. As the city of Calgary grew, the phosphate in the increasing volume of effluent entering the Bow began to stimulate the growth of submerged aquatic plants to a dangerous degree. The photosynthetic process of plants causes them to use oxygen at night and release it in the day. Plant growth was so heavy in the Bow that dissolved oxygen levels became very low in the early morning hours. In addition to nighttime oxygen depletion, the organic matter present in the effluent further robbed the water of oxygen when it decomposed. Together these factors caused the concentration of dissolved oxygen to fluctuate wildly each day during the summer growing season. Oxygen levels ranged from 45–170 percent of saturation, and readings as low as 2.7 parts per million were recorded in the mid-1960s. Fish become stressed when dissolved oxygen levels drop to between 3 and 4 parts per million.

At that time it was additionally noted that the numbers and types of insects living in the river above Calgary were substantially different from those below the city. Mayflies and stoneflies, for instance, were absent from the insect regime immediately below the city but made a remarkable comeback by the time the river reached Carseland, 40 miles (64 km) downstream. In addition the Bow above Calgary supported a wide variety of insects with relatively few individuals of each type, while the river below produced few genera but large numbers of individuals in those genera. Biologists now recognize this condition as a classic indicator of severe organic pollution.

In 1968, at a point near Policeman's Crossing, phosphate concentrations between .71 and 2 parts per million were registered. The normal level in the Bow above Calgary was .15 parts per million, 5–13 times lower. In August 1967 depleted oxygen levels in the river combined with an industrial waste discharge of ammonia to produce in a fish kill affecting rainbow trout and whitefish in the Bow between Fish Creek and Carseland. The combined factors of the rapid growth of the city, the changing ecology of the river and the potential for industrial discharge were threatening the future of the fishery.

Secondary sewage treatment, which became a nationwide issue in the late 1960s, was initiated in Calgary at the Bonnybrook treatment plant in 1970 in an effort to improve water quality in the Bow. Secondary treatment is a process that removes most of the oxygen-depleting substances from the effluent but releases what is in effect a liquid fertilizer rich in phosphate and nitrate.

The impact of secondary treatment on the river was immediate and positive. A water quality study completed in 1972–73 noted an increase in the level of dissolved oxygen coupled with decreases in bacteriological constituents (including coliform bacteria) and biochemical oxygen demand constituents (organic materials that use oxygen when they decompose). The study concluded that "the river did not suffer markedly from the pollution load imposed on it."

Through the 1970s the city of Calgary rode the oil business through an economic boom. Its population swelled from about 385,000 in 1970 to 560,000 in 1980, a 45 percent increase in just a decade. The resulting increase in the municipal effluent volume entering the river caused the water quality to deteriorate gradually to presecondary treatment conditions. Weed growth returned to the prolific levels witnessed in the early 1960s. The phosphorous entering the river stimulated plant growth to the point that algae grew

100 times faster in water taken from below the Bonnybrook treatment plant than in water taken from above. In 1978 it was estimated that the river downstream of Calgary held 72 tons of aquatic plants per mile (44 metric tons per kilometer).

It is thought that the dissolved oxygen problems very nearly caused catastrophic fish kills on a couple of occasions. In the hot, dry summer of 1979 increased irrigation demands, low oxygen levels in the early morning hours and water temperatures as high as 78°F (25.5°C) had regional fisheries Biologist Bill Griffiths very concerned. It appeared the river was again being pushed closer and closer to the brink of disaster. No one knew, however, how much the fishery could be stressed before fish kills occurred. Fortunately the river made it through the summer without disaster.

So once again the circle was complete. Secondary treatment had solved the water quality problem temporarily, but as the city grew, the increasing volume of effluent brought a return of the same old problems. In 1980, facing mounting public pressure, Alberta Environment undertook a large-scale study to quantify the problem of overenrichment in the Bow River and to determine if phosphate removal facilities at sewage treatment plants would improve water quality. As a result, in 1982 phosphate removal was initiated at both the Bonnybrook and Fish Creek sewage treatment plants, reducing phosphorous loadings in the effluent by an estimated 75 percent. The volume of plant growth in the river has consequently decreased even in low water years.

Throughout the recurring cycle of effluent increases leading to fluctuations in dissolved oxygen content, the river has nevertheless continued to produce trout in large numbers and of large average size. Nothing more than good fortune allowed this to be the case because the river was not deemed worthy of special investigation as a trout fishery until the early 1980s. Prior to that time few people other than a small number of anglers and biologists voiced concern over the effect the deteriorating water quality was having on the trout. Fortunately the steps taken by the city and province to eradicate the water quality problems were also the steps necessary to preserve the fishery—yet another case of the fishery being the unintentional benefactor of human manipulation. The restorative measures initiated by the city's self-interest were just what were needed to protect the trout as well.

The trout fishery of the middle Bow River, then, truly is a magnificent accident. Paradoxically the river's proximity to the city of Calgary has allowed it to reach its full potential, and yet that proximity also has periodically presented it with the greatest threats to its survival. The river has, with a healthy dose of good fortune and some enlightened fisheries management in recent years, shown a remarkably resilient character in beating the odds and remaining a world-class trout stream.

4

The Bow
River Trout
Fishery Today

IF YOU WERE TO CREATE a standard against which sport fisheries could be judged, a sort of piscatorial performance review, you'd give marks for the following qualities: the population of fish, the size of fish, the variety of fish species, the variety of types of fishing and the aesthetics of the river environment. On such a report card most of the Bow River from Banff to Bassano would warrant the highest possible grade.

The upper Bow today carries a healthy population of brown trout, mountain whitefish and brook trout down as far as its confluence with the Kananaskis River. Between there and the Bearspaw dam the river is less productive and less appealing. The power dams in this section of river still cause severe fluctuations in water level, making the river a poorer fish habitat.

From Bearspaw down to well below Carseland the sport fishery is dominated by whitefish and rainbow and brown trout, with browns being somewhat more common near Calgary. The most recent population estimates for the river below Calgary were completed in 1992, and they put the combined population of brown and rainbow trout of catchable size—meaning over 6 inches (15 cm) long—at about 3,033 per mile (1,850 per km).

The growth rate of fish in the Bow below Calgary equals or exceeds that of fish in most other high-quality trout streams, including the Madison, Bighorn and Battenkill. Consequently the average size of fish taken by anglers is larger on this part of the Bow than on most other rivers. A Bow River fish four years of age is approximately 19 inches (48 cm) long, while one from the Madison is about 16 inches (41 cm).

One interesting difference between this part of the Bow and some of the West's other fine trout streams is the frequency with which fly-fishers encounter mountain whitefish. I fished the Bow for 10 years before I caught a whitefish, so naturally I presumed there weren't many. When the first population studies were completed in 1980, though, biologists found huge numbers of them in the Bow downstream of Calgary. The fish are actively pursued in the city by bait-fishers, but fly-fishers catch them infrequently in spite of their abundance, a puzzle for which I have no explanation. On the Madison and Missouri rivers in Montana, the Henry's Fork in Idaho or even the Crowsnest in southern Alberta, anglers often catch far more whitefish than trout, and at times they become quite a nuisance.

The river below Calgary still produces the very occasional cutthroat or rainbow–cutthroat hybrid. Some scientists believe that all Bow River rainbows are really hybrids. The occasional bull trout is caught below Calgary as well, and in fact the largest fish taken in a 1981 population study was a huge bull trout about 30 inches (76 cm) long that was too much for the biologists' 9-pound (4-kg) scale.

One of the many critical links in the continuance of a wild trout fishery is the availability of suitable spawning grounds, and in this regard the Bow is fortunate. All species of sport fish have suitable spawning water available to them either in the main river or its tributaries.

The brown and brook trout in the upper river spawn in side channels of the Bow and in small tributaries like Bill Griffiths Creek (named in honor of the late regional biologist).

The rainbows of the middle Bow spawn primarily in the streams of the Highwood River system, migrating there starting in early April and returning to the Bow in late May and June. Fish also spawn in the Highwood's major tributary, the Sheep River, and its numerous small, clean, gravel-bottomed tributaries that flow east out of the foothills. Bow River fish have been observed spawning as far as 60 miles (100 km) from the mouth of the Highwood. Some rainbow trout spawning also takes place in the Bow itself in the 9 miles (14 km) of river downstream of the Bearspaw dam.

I suppose the journey of a Bow River rainbow trout to its spawning grounds is not as dramatic or soul stirring as that of anadromous fish such as Pacific salmon or steelhead, but I nevertheless take pleasure in knowing that rainbow trout spawn within a short distance of my home. I feel a strong sense of admiration and something resembling fatherly pride.

The farther up the tributaries the fish go, the smaller the streams become and the more vulnerable fish are to both human and natural predation. After all, a 4–5-pound (1.8–2.3-kg) rainbow has a hard time remaining inconspicuous in a creek barely big enough to turn around in. As a consequence the entire Highwood system remains closed to angling until June 16 to protect these fish.

Rainbows are generally three to four years of age when they first spawn. Most of the adult fish return from the tributaries fairly promptly after spawning, but the newly hatched fry most often spend their first year in the smaller streams, moving down to the Bow in the midsummer of the following year.

Both brown trout and mountain whitefish spawn in autumn. The browns start when the water temperature drops below 50°F (10°C), which often occurs about mid-October. Almost all the brown trout that live below Calgary spawn within the city of Calgary in the Bow itself and in the Elbow between its confluence with the Bow and the Glenmore dam. Whitefish also spawn throughout the Bow and in the Highwood and its tributaries.

Though the healthy size of Bow River trout has remained a constant throughout the years, the river today is in many ways a different river than the one I fished for the first time as a teenager in 1970. It's even a somewhat different river than the one I wrote about in the first edition of this book in 1987. The primary difference is that the number of anglers has continued to grow, and the fish have become harder to catch. I now consider the river below Calgary to be difficult for anglers to become familiar with quickly. It's not unusual to see fly-rodders with a great deal of experience on other streams initially having a great deal of trouble on the Bow.

In the early days of the guiding industry we often wondered how long the fishery below Calgary could last, for to that point it owed its existence mainly to good luck. Given the rapid growth of the city, the city's apparent disregard for the health of the fishery and the province's obsession with increased development and irrigation, it was easy to expect the worst. It wasn't hard to imagine a city of one million people, a river dammed for irrigation, polluted by municipal sewage and industrial discharge, and big trout nothing more than a memory.

But the Bow is still a great trout river, and perhaps that is no longer because of exceptional luck, but because of the efforts of people who use and love the river. The river's fame has multiplied the number who count themselves as friends of the Bow. I believe that these friends will continue to be invaluable, even crucial, to the preservation of the river in the future. The late Lee Wulff, the godfather of trout streams, put it this way:

A river that is only fished by a few people, under attack by pollution or something else, doesn't have defenders. But a river that is loved and used by a great many people has a great many defenders and a great strength.

CHAPTER

5

Fishing the Bow River

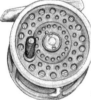

WHATEVER your angling preferences, the Bow has a way to satisfy them. If the setting in which you fish is the most critical part of the experience, then the upper river, perhaps in Banff National Park, is where you will be found. If you're a big-fish hunter you'll skulk around at night within Calgary or slam a saltwater-sized streamer into the brushy banks below Carseland. If you are more comfortable fishing small, intimate streams, you might be found near one of the islands that break the river up into side channels that can be fished much like small streams. Such channels are particularly abundant on the upper river near Canmore and just upstream of the Carseland weir. And though trout might be your usual quarry, the lower reaches of the river also offer angling for pike, walleye and goldeye.

Bow River trout can be caught with a variety of tackle, but the river fulfills its potential best as a fly-fishing stream. In my thirty years on the river I've never wanted to use spinning or spin-casting tackle. It could be argued that any method of angling will to a greater or lesser degree provide the thrill that comes from being connected to a wild, fighting fish. If the thrill is the objective it doesn't matter what method is employed to achieve it.

For me, though, the real objective of fishing is an understanding of what is going on in the fish's world, and fly-fishing is simply the most entertaining means of furthering that understanding. I may, for example, through experience and observation come to believe rising trout are feeding on a certain stage of a certain insect. The results of my fishing with an imitation of that insect will confirm or contradict my belief.

In a like manner, when fish aren't rising I speculate on what foods may be available to them under the surface according to the time of year, the time of day, the type of water and my knowledge of the insect life in that particular stream. Then I try to imitate what the trout are seeing with my choice of fly and fishing method.

My desire to understand the fish's world, of course, is presumptuous, for such understanding is never complete and therefore never certain. Fly-fishing is deliciously more complicated than that. My analysis may be correct, but my imitation and presentation may not be good enough to fool the fish. On the other hand, even if I'm wrong about what the fish are feeding on, they may take my fly because it triggers some instinctual response for which I have no explanation. In this case I am unaware that I have analyzed the situation incorrectly and am patting myself on the back undeservedly.

It is the inevitability of uncertainty in fly-fishing that appeals to me. A behavioral psychologist once told me that human beliefs are strengthened most by random or partial reinforcements. This must be why, like so many other fly-rodders, I am fascinated with trout behavior: I am never able to figure it out all the time.

TACKLE

In the good old days before the Bow River's popularity became widespread, fly-rodders could choose a method—dry flies or streamers—and stay with it, knowing it would probably work somewhere between reasonably well and very well just about every day. Today, however, it rarely pays to stubbornly pursue one method all day long.

Today's successful Bow River fly-fisher is versatile and lets the fish dictate the method. Since it's not uncommon to cast tiny dry flies and enormous streamers on the same day, some care must be taken in choosing tackle. One option is to pick a versatile outfit, say an 8½- or 9-foot 6-weight that will provide both the finesse and power required to fish the river. A second approach is to have two outfits ready—one a gentle 8- or 8½-foot 4- or 5-weight for the touchy small-fly stuff and the other a beefy 9-foot 7- or 8-weight for the full-contact streamer fishing the Bow also offers. The latter approach is usually favored by anglers who float the river because it's easy to carry a second outfit in the boat. Those who fish from their feet usually prefer to carry one versatile outfit. Though the Bow is a big river with big fish, other fly-rodders opt to go in search of rising fish with a dainty 2- or 3-weight outfit. I confess a bias toward this myself. Finally, although the average wind speed at Calgary is only about 10 miles (16 km) per hour, the breeze can occasionally become a problem, so crisp, fast-action rods, which develop higher line speeds and cast tighter loops, are often favored.

The choice of fly line depends on the speed and depth of the water and the type of fly. All dry flies and most nymphs are fished on the Bow with floating lines. Streamers can be fished on floating lines, too, but most streamer specialists prefer a 10- or 15-foot sink-tip line with a front end that sinks very quickly.

A good, smooth spring-and-pawl or disc-drag fly reel is need-ed on the Bow because this is one of very few trout streams where the drag system will be tested severely. The fighting quality of Bow River fish, particularly the rainbow trout, is something local anglers take for granted. Visitors, however, are quick to point out that these trout are among the hardest fighting anywhere. I vividly recall fish-ing with Dr. Charles Oyer one September when he had trout take all his fly line and part of his backing 15 times in two days. On another occasion, while shooting some videotape on the Bow, I had a fish take an ant pattern about 20 feet (6 m) from me, then run nearly 300 feet (91 m) straight across the river before jumping at the far bank. Guides frequently pile everybody hastily into a driftboat to follow a fish an angler has hooked while wading off the tail of an island. No less an authority than the late A.J. McClane, writing in *Sports Afield,* declared

> *These fish have more bounce to the ounce. The four and five-pounders wheel into the current and get into your backing like bonefish, and everybody who visits the stream is impressed by their stamina. As much as I delight in catching rainbows in the Yellow-stone and Madison, those fish just aren't in the same league.*

The lesson in all this? Put some backing on your reel. You're going to need it.

METHODS

Streamer Fishing

A streamer was originally defined as a feather-winged fly tied to imitate a small fish. Another category of fly that imitates a fish is known as a bucktail because it has a wing made of animal hair. Today though, most people group feather-winged streamers and hair-winged bucktails under the generic term of streamers. Also falling into this category by default are imitations of leeches.

The fry of three species of suckers—longnose, mountain and white—have been identified in the Bow system, and these are important trout foods. As well, fathead minnows, lake chub, long-nose dace and trout–perch are baitfish that have been sampled in the river both above and below Calgary. A species of sculpin min-now, the spoonhead, is reported to inhabit both the upper and mid-dle river. I have found specimens near the Inglewood Bird Sanctu-ary in Calgary, but I have not seen any below the city. Sculpins are an important food for large trout because they are less than nimble and can be easily caught when the current sweeps them out from under rocks and boulders. Adult trout, of course, are indiscriminate in their pursuit of small fish, and their menu lists more than just baitfish or nonsport fish. Big browns or rainbows are opportunistic and will eat any small fish they think they can get their mouths around.

Leeches form an important food for Bow River trout as well, particularly in the stretch below Calgary. Leeches can reach 4–5 inches (10–13 cm) in length and vary in color from black to grey to deep reddish brown. It's not uncommon for a captured fish to regurgitate a number of these ugly creatures while the angler unhooks and releases it.

Bow River streamer anglers usually take an impressionistic approach to fly pattern, opting for those that generally resemble several food items rather than those that exactly imitate one species. Many favorite patterns have marabou feathers in the dressing, and these include the Bow River Bugger and Marabou Muddler. As well, Matuka streamers and flies using rabbit fur for wings, like the Zonker series, are also highly regarded by both fish and fly-fishers. Fly popularity seems to move in cycles on the Bow, and flies that have ridden the crest at one time or another are the Marabou Leech, Marabou Dace and more recently the Gander and Clouser Minnow.

Of course more than just style determines the effectiveness of a fly. There's the quality of presentation, and beyond that there's the intangible effect of the confidence of presentation. What often makes a fly a favorite is the fact that the angler expects it to work. When fishing a fly with confidence, an angler usually concentrates harder and as a result fishes more effectively.

No matter what tackle is used, the first step in attempting to catch fish is to figure out where they are holding. Trout require three things to survive in moving water: shelter from heavy current, safety from predators (those in and out of the water) and access to food. The best fish-holding places, known as prime lies, exist where all three factors are present. I always told clients I was guiding to look for seams in the river. These can be locations where fast water meets slow, where deep water meets shallow or where flat water meets broken. One of the most productive areas in a big river like the Bow is along the banks. If the water there is moving, is more than 18 inches (46 cm) deep and has some cover, fish will probably be holding there, where they have both shelter and relief from the current. Biologists' electrofishing experience confirms these places as ones where trout concentrate.

Many people are not aware that fish in moving water have no choice but to face into the current (so water will enter their mouths and exit their gills rather than the reverse), and this should be taken advantage of by fly-fishers when approaching potential holding water.

One fundamental of streamer fishing is always to allow the current to take the fly to the fish. Don't merely cast the fly directly at the spot where you think fish are holding. Trout are used to seeing the current bring their food to them, so streamers should enter the scene the same way. You should usually take a position upstream and across from the expected lie of the fish. The cast is then made across, and as the current carries the fly downstream, use the rod to steer the fly across and through the fishy area. Strikes normally occur as the fly starts to swing across the current, so naturally you try to arrange for the fly to be in good water when it starts to swing.

Variations on this basic technique are endless. You can throw a large loop of line (called a mend) upstream immediately after casting to allow the fly to sink deeper and move across the current more slowly. You can allow the fly to swing around downstream of the casting position with no motion other than that imparted by the current, or you can introduce some extra action varying from subtle twitches of the rod tip to pumping movements to frantic retrieves as fast as the line can be stripped in.

A second fundamental of streamer fishing is to be aware of how deep the fly is sinking. The most succinct appraisal of wet-fly fishing I have ever heard came from Charlie Brooks, who contended that most of the time the difference between good and average wet-fly anglers is nothing more than the depth at which they fish their flies. In rough, broken water the shelter from current exists on the stream bottom in pockets of still water behind big rocks. If you are not catching fish or snagging your flies on the rocks periodically, it may be wise to get the fly deeper, which can be accomplished in several ways. In addition to making a mend as soon as the fly lands, you can give the fly more time to sink before it starts to swing by casting to a spot far upstream of the expected lie of the fish. You also can switch to a sinking line, weighted streamer or both, or add some weight to the leader a few inches above the fly.

Adherence to three principles will simplify casting large or heavily weighted flies. First, cast a wide loop so the fly can't catch on the line during the cast. Second, be sure to wait for the back cast to straighten out completely before starting the forward cast. Third, never underpower either the back or forward cast. If you don't put enough force into the cast the fly will drop as it travels, usually to just about head height—which brings me to a corollary rule: always wear glasses when fly-fishing. You are only allotted one set of eyes per lifetime. Polarized glasses are best because they cut glare from the surface of the water and help you spot fish and locate holes in the stream bottom.

When fishing with a sinking line, it is best to use a very short leader. Any fly, even a weighted one, is inclined to rise in the water when held against the current, and a long leader will allow the fly to ride a couple of feet above the end of the fly line. A leader 4 feet (1.2 m) or less in length will ensure that the fly stays as deep as the end of the fly line and will also make it easier to cast a heavily weighted fly. Lefty Kreh showed me this trick, and to prove his point he successfully used a leader about 4 inches (10 cm) long to fish streamers on the Bow.

Bow River fly-rodders' versatile methods extend to fishing two streamers together, a technique I've seen nowhere else. The first fly is tied to the leader in the normal fashion and the second is tied to a 2-foot (61-cm) piece of tippet material attached to the bend of the first. The trailing fly is usually smaller and a different color than the first. The advantage of this rig is that you can try different colors and sizes of flies simultaneously; the disadvantage is that you can develop tennis elbow from casting it too long.

Streamer fishing has other hazards as my friend Russ Thornberry found out. He was standing with his back to a high, grassy bank while pitching a big streamer across a side channel. He leaned into an underwear-tearing forward cast only to find that his fly had caught on something behind him. He turned around in time to see the world's unluckiest skunk tumbling down the bank toward him with a #2 Woolly Bugger through his nose.

Dry-Fly Fishing

If I asked fly-fishers to name their favorite type of trout fishing, I believe 90 percent would name dry-fly fishing. Dry-fly fishing has all the elements of a good adventure: optimism, planning, action, suspense, climax. It is the most visual type of fly-fishing and therefore is the method that gives anglers the most direct, tangible contact with their quarry.

Dry-fly fishing on the Bow River can be divided into two categories: fishing the water (or "fishing blind") and fishing to rising fish. Flies that work well for fishing the water are sometimes called searching patterns. These are high-floating, hair-winged flies such as Humpys, Royal Wulffs and Stimulators. They are cast above the expected lie of the fish and allowed to drift downstream drag-free. You usually fish your way upstream, putting the fly through each potential holding spot five or six times before moving to the next good pocket. Fishing the water is relaxing and readily allows for the thoughtful introspection that fly-fishing has long been known to nurture. After fishing up the river for a while it's not uncommon to suddenly realize you have no idea how long you've been fishing, how far you've moved upstream or even what time it is. Then you'll remember that this is precisely the reason for going fishing.

Fishing to rising fish is the fly-fisher's chess match, for it involves plenty of strategy, planning and execution. The procedure is to find a rising fish, determine what insect it is eating, select a suitable imitation and finally deliver it in a convincing manner. The varying combinations of factors that go into successful dry-fly fishing make for very interesting, almost cerebral sport. It also prompts fly-fishers to keep records of their trips so they can understand the sequence of insect hatches on their favorite streams and know in future what to expect before they arrive at the water.

The tackle for dry-fly fishing on the Bow River is matched to the size of flies being used. Hoppers and other large dries are best handled with rods that cast 6- or 7-weight lines. Smaller flies are best fished with 4- or 5-weight lines. Leaders for dry-fly fishing are usually around 9 feet (3 m) long with the tippet diameter matched to the fly size via the rule of four. The fly size is divided by four, and the result is the "x" designation for the tippet diameter. For example, a #16 fly would require a tippet diameter of 4x, which is .007 inches in diameter. This is a general rule, and anglers will often deviate $^1/1000$th of an inch either way from this figure, depending on conditions.

Some anglers (usually very conscientious visitors who have been made gun-shy by the finicky trout of Silver Creek or the Henry's Fork) try to use leaders as fine as 6x or 7x on the Bow. Such fine leaders, however, don't work very well on the Bow because the fish are simply too strong. Fly-rodders find this out soon enough, and when they do it's usually good for a few laughs and some chiding from a guide or fishing partner.

Fishing with grasshopper imitations from late July through late September is a special pleasure on the Bow. Bow River trout, even the big ones, consider a chunky hopper well worth searching for. Hoppers are abundant in the grass along the river's edge, so the fish learn to expect them near the bank rather than midstream. For years Alberta's favorite grasshopper imitation has been the Letort Hopper, a Pennsylvania pattern popularized locally by Red Deer outdoor writer Bob Scammell. Recently though, anglers have also been experimenting successfully with more complex flies like the Dave's Hopper and Whit's Hopper.

Nymph Fishing

In recent years, when I've really felt like fishing aggressively rather than systematically working a streamer or waiting for rising fish to appear, I've taken to nymph fishing. Nymph fishing has long been described as the most consistently effective method for taking trout in streams. It is also considered the most difficult method to learn because it carries an inherent contradiction: confidence in the method is required to make it successful, but success is needed to build this confidence. I don't think nymph fishing is particularly difficult, but it does require stubborn perseverance on the part of the angler.

An artificial nymph is a fly that imitates the immature or pre-adult stage of an aquatic insect. Though the Bow's individual species vary substantially from the headwaters to the mouth, the important insects throughout are the same as those found on most other western trout streams: mayflies, stoneflies and caddisflies. Within each order are many species that vary widely in size, color and behavior. Stoneflies, for instance, are common throughout the river, but they vary in size from about ⅜ inch (10 mm) to about 2 inches (50 mm).

On the Bow I usually prefer to use impressionistic nymphs that are buggy enough to represent several different insects. My favorite stonefly nymphs are the Charles Brooks patterns: the Montana Stone and the Yellow Stone. For imitating mayfly and caddisfly nymphs I like the Pheasant Tail and various sizes and colors of the Gold-Ribbed Hare's Ear in both bead-head and standard versions.

In the late 1980s the fly known as the San Juan Worm began to cause quite a stir among Bow River anglers. Named for the trout river in New Mexico where it was developed, it represents a—well, a worm—but a legitimate worm, if you will, that lives in the weeds and silt of the Bow River downstream of Calgary. Though technically not a nymph, it's fished with the same method. It's a natural trout food, and it makes perfect sense to try to imitate it, for there are times when it outfishes almost everything else. Though it is difficult for some purists to be comfortable using a fly with the word *worm* in its name, eventually even the staunchest protesters succumb to its charm, finding it hard to maintain their prejudices when everybody around them is catching fish like mad.

One of the most knowledgeable of nymph fishermen was the late Charles Brooks of West Yellowstone, Montana. He wrote several books on fly-fishing western waters, and they all emphasize nymph fishing. His favorite method was developed for fishing large stonefly nymphs in the fast, choppy water of the Madison River.

The method calls for a fast-sinking fly line, a short 0x or 1x leader and a #4 or 6 heavily weighted nymph. The fly-fisher takes a position upstream of the spot where fish are thought to be holding and makes a short cast up and across stream. The fly is carried downstream by the current, and the rod is gradually raised to take up the accumulating slack. Ideally the fly should be on the stream bottom as it reaches a point directly across from angler. As the nymph moves downstream, the rod is gradually lowered to allow the fly to continue to drift near the bottom. It is at this stage that the take—felt as a light, sharp tap—usually occurs. The angler must strike quickly to hook the fish through the slack line.

The Bow River contains much water suited to Charlie's method, and when he fished the river in 1979, he told me he could happily spend a whole day on one 200-yard stretch of water I showed him. At one point, after demonstrating his technique, he sat on the bank and suggested that I give it a try with his rod. I complied eagerly and eventually caught a nice trout. The experience completed a circle for me, for I was very much a Charlie Brooks disciple. To use his rod, his Yellow Stone Nymph and his method on my river—with him watching—is a treasured memory in my fishing career.

Another nymphing method particularly effective for imitating emerging mayflies and caddisflies is the simple down-and-across wet-fly method. The fly is cast quartering downstream on a floating line and allowed to swing in the current. You add various subtle movements with the rod tip to mimic the swimming action of the nymph. The cast is planned so the fly will start to rise against the tension of the line just before it reaches the fish's feeding station.

The nymph fishing method most popular today on the Bow requires a floating fly line, a leader about 9 feet (3 m) long and a strike indicator. A strike indicator is a brightly colored marker attached to the leader a few feet above the fly. The angler uses it as a visual reference point and watches for it to move erratically when a fish takes the nymph. Many different materials can be used as indicators: pieces of fluorescent yarn, short pieces of brightly colored fly line or round, painted "corkies." I also sometimes use a leader with the butt section dyed fluorescent red or orange.

This type of nymph fishing can be very accurately described as dry-fly fishing underwater because it shares the important objective of avoiding drag on the fly. The inherent problem, however, is that the fly is underwater and can't be seen. Consequently you must determine from the drift of the line and leader whether the fly is behaving properly. The fly is cast upstream, and as it drifts back toward you, the rod and line are manipulated to avoid drag. The rod is usually held high to keep most of the fly line off of the water so it can't be caught by currents that could produce unnatural movement of the fly. The method puts a high priority on control, and casts of longer than 30 feet (9 m) are impractical.

The beauty of nymph fishing with a strike indicator is its versatility. It can be used in nearly every type of water, and it is effective for everything from #4 stonefly nymphs to #18 or 20 mayfly nymphs. It can be used when fishing the water blind, when fishing over visible nymphing fish or when sight-casting to fish holding on the stream bottom. Because it requires the same tackle as dry-fly fishing, the switch from one method to another is quick and simple.

Some of the best places to fish a nymph and indicator on the Bow are in side channels, where the holding water can be identified easily and covered efficiently. Other areas suited to this method are depressions in the river bottom. Each winter the ice carves and gouges the gravel, leaving deep spots in some riffles. The riffle itself may be 1–2 feet (30–61 cm) deep with the depression only a little deeper, but these zones usually hold fish. A nymph properly drifted through the depression will often encourage them to strike.

One such depression a few miles downstream of the Highway 22x bridge has held fish for many years. When I was guiding it was the surest place I knew of for a client to hook a trout. Even when the whole river was turned off, we could still count on this spot, and for the first five years I knew about it we were never shut out as long as the water was clear. The spot has come to be known as the guidemaker and has been responsible for some big tips from clients who thought their guide was a genius.

Of course guides will go to extreme lengths to convince their clients they are endowed with mystical, magical gifts that make them better than any other guide. They also take advantage of anything they can to perpetuate this myth, including the practice of catch-and-release angling.

One year a rainbow trout measuring exactly 19 ⅜ inches lived in a small side channel. He was identifiable because of a peculiar deformity on his lower jaw, and I had clients catch him several times through the summer. One fisherman got quite excited when he hooked the fish and allowed that it looked like a pretty good trout—maybe 21 or 22 inches. "Naw," I said, "it looks like about 19 ⅜ inches to me." After the trout was landed and measured, the angler looked at me in a most peculiar manner, and for the rest of his trip did *everything* I suggested.

The nymph and strike indicator method is likewise ideal for catching whitefish on a fly, especially on the Highwood River and its tributaries, which host enormous runs of these fish in the autumn. The whitefish seem especially fond of a small Pheasant Tail Nymph or a South Platte Brassie. I don't kill trout from wild fisheries, but on occasion I like to take some mountain whitefish home for the smoker, and until the season closes October 31, they can provide good fun and some fine eating.

It's common and fairly easy on the Bow River to fish two nymphs together because the river bottom is relatively free of debris. The nymphs can be rigged in a number of different ways, but the one I prefer is simply to connect the flies eye-to-eye with a piece of leader material 12–18 inches (30–46 cm) long and then tie the larger fly to the end of the leader.

Another popular two-fly method on the Bow River is to fish a nymph and a dry fly together. A high-floating dry like a hopper or Stimulator serves as both fly and strike indicator for the smaller nymph below. The method has both benefits and drawbacks. It allows you to experiment with two flies simultaneously, and it's especially useful when you're floating the river because the two-fly rig helps compensate for the fact that you only get one shot at each prime spot as you drift by. But the method prevents you from fishing either fly as well as you could if you were using it alone. The rig also is difficult to cast and prone to tangles. But if you don't use too big a nymph and don't separate the nymph and the dry fly by more than a couple of feet, the hopper-dropper can be a good trick to have up your sleeve.

PLAYING THE FISH

One fundamental skill demanded of Bow River fly-rodders is the ability to play large fish properly once they have been hooked. Many visiting anglers have never encountered trout capable of taking any fly line off the reel, let alone taking *all* the line off the reel. When their first big Bow rainbow takes the fly, they invariably look down at the reel, see nothing but a smoking blur, decide the picture can't be correct, make a frantic grab at the reel handle and break either the leader or their knuckles or both. Such scenes are always a dilemma for guides, for no matter how carefully they explain beforehand what anglers should expect of Bow River trout, they rarely follow the advice. If guides try to coach anglers in the heat of battle, things turn even worse. Anglers are by then fighting the biggest fish of their life, and the last thing they are going to do is pay attention to someone screaming instructions in their ear. In all likelihood, after the excitement dies down, the frustrated guides will ask, "Why didn't you do what I said?" To which the frazzled anglers will reply, "Did you say something?" I eventually learned to let clients do whatever they wanted with the first fish while I enjoyed the show. Later, when the shaking was over, I'd casually make some suggestions on how to handle these big, fast-running fish, which is basically to play them from the reel, let them run when they want to and pressure them when they stop to rest.

FLOATING THE RIVER

The Bow River's size makes float or drift trips a popular way to fish for a number of reasons. A boat allows access to the entire river in the section being floated: both banks and all islands and side channels. The water too deep to wade, especially the outsides of bends, becomes accessible from a boat, and flies such as grasshopper or adult stonefly patterns can be more effectively fished because of the long, drag-free floats that are possible from a boat.

The Bow is a big but reasonably safe river with enough access points in the Banff–Seebee and Calgary–Carseland sections to allow a number of different day trips or overnight excursions. Drifting the river is a unique experience. You'll find that the current moves you along at a perfect speed to view the sights. The scenery changes constantly but not so quickly that you can't take it all in. The silence of your movement allows a surprisingly close approach to wildlife. On cooler, late season mornings the river valley is often enveloped in fog, which can be a photographer's dream.

There's no doubt that the best way to see the Bow in full splendor is to spend two or three days floating and camping. At night you notice sounds you weren't aware of in the daytime: the hum of swarming caddisflies, the gabble of unseen ducks and geese, and the occasional slosh of a boldly feeding trout.

Certain precautions need to be taken when planning a float trip. First, you must be certain your craft and your skills are matched to the water you will be drifting—you won't make it through the Class VI white water above Banff in a cartopper. Second, *know where and how far away the takeout point is.* Familiarize yourself with landmarks, and don't put yourself in the position of having to find the takeout spot in the dark. I was fishing the Bow above the Highwood junction one time when a boat drifted by me just as the sun was setting. One of the people in the boat hollered across, "How far to Carseland?" I don't think they believed me when I called back, "About 25 miles." Equally confused was the couple drifting by me a few miles *downstream* of the mouth of the Highwood River who wanted to know how far it was to the river's mouth. I told them it was a *long* way if they kept going in their present direction.

When planning a float trip, the best way to solve the logistical problems of putting in and taking out the boat is to make all vehicle moves prior to the trip. This way your pickup vehicle will be at the takeout point whenever you get there, even if you are inordinately late. Another option is to have a couple of friends move your vehicle for you, but should there be some miscommunication, you may experience a sinking feeling when you drift up to the takeout point at dark to find that your vehicle isn't there. I am more familiar with this feeling than I would choose to be, but in one case at least it had a positive side. I floated the river with outdoor writers Lefty Kreh and Bob Scammell, and while we awaited the arrival of my truck, Lefty proceeded to relate every joke and funny story known to the English language. If I close my eyes I can still see Lefty and Bob silhouetted in the moonlight, laughing and peeing into the darkness.

An option to be avoided if you value matrimonial harmony and friendship is having someone meet you at the takeout point at a prescribed time. You are a fly-fisher and you will be late. One last piece of advice: make sure you've got your car keys before you push the boat away from the bank.

A better option is to engage the services of one of the people who make a summer business of moving vehicles for guides and anglers fishing the Bow below Calgary. Their service is reliable and inexpensive, and contact with them can be made through tackle shops in Calgary.

Those who float and camp must be aware that the Bow flows through three different classifications of land—national park, Indian reserve and private property—with different regulations for camping in each. In Banff National Park, for example, camping is allowed only in designated campgrounds, which rules out the possibility of an isolated wilderness experience along the banks of the river. Camping on Indian reserves requires a permit, and setting up your tent on private land requires permission of the landowner. Islands in sections of the river not flowing through the Indian reserves or the national park, however, are Crown land, and camping is legal. But the onus is always on anglers to determine the status of the land where they intend to camp.

Campers shouldn't be tempted to drink the water from the Bow (or any stream or lake in Alberta for that matter). Though much of the water from high-altitude streams and lakes would not hurt, there is no surface water in the province that meets stringent potability standards.

Boats

The type of craft to be used on the river will depend on the nature of the trip and the type of water on the portion of river you will be floating. If you want to fish while drifting, then a boat is what you want, provided that the section of water you've chosen is navigable. If you want good maneuverability and wish only to use the craft to move from one fishing spot to another, then a canoe is ideal.

For the first several years that I floated the middle Bow, I used a plain 12-foot aluminum cartop boat. It seemed fine at the time, but looking back I don't know how I managed with three people and all their gear. The boat was definitely crowded. Anglers had virtually no place to put their feet, and if the one in the stern seat leaned back too far, he got the butt end of an oar in the back. A small cartopper should be considered acceptable for a maximum of two people as long as the water is of a gentle nature, as it is between Calgary and Carseland. The 14-foot version of the same aluminum boat is a reasonable choice for up to three people though conditions will still be a little crowded.

At one time the boat most commonly used on the middle river by serious fly-fishers and guides was the flat-bottomed aluminum boat called a johnboat. It is available in a couple of different hull designs and in 12-, 14-, 16- and 18-foot lengths. The 12-footer is too small for more than two people, so most guides used the wide-beamed 14-foot lake johnboat. Eric Grinnell, an outfitter who guides on the Bow below Carseland, is referred to as the Commodore for his fleet of 16- and 18-footers. At times he even sets up a propane stove and lawn chairs in his boats, and cooks a lunch on the fly while moving between fishing spots. He says it saves valuable fishing time.

The great majority of my Bow River float trips over the years have been taken in a 14-foot lake john. It's a reasonably comfortable and convenient boat, fitting in the back of a full-size pickup truck or on a car roof rack. As well, at a weight of about 150 pounds (68 kg), it can be carried short distances by two or three people, making it possible to move it to and from the water in places where a heavier boat isn't feasible. Swivel seats can easily be installed to elevate the anglers and make them more comfortable.

The most popular boat on the Bow River today is the McKenzie River driftboat, which was designed for the swift coastal rivers of Oregon and Washington. It's a strange-looking boat, built high at both ends, much like an oceangoing dory. McKenzie driftboats are well-suited to navigating rough water, even white water, though they are difficult to handle in a stiff wind. They are equipped with knee braces to allow anglers to stand while fishing, and many are outfitted with dry storage areas to protect gear from rain and bilgewater. McKenzie River driftboats, however, are expensive and heavy, and must be trailered. They also are more difficult to get in and out of than johnboats.

Yet another option for floating the Bow River is an inflatable boat of the sort used frequently on Wyoming and Idaho rivers. Inflatables, of course, are light and highly portable. But they are difficult to handle in the winds that often blow in the Bow Valley, and anglers can't stand while fishing.

The recently developed one-person inflatable represents another alternative. Called a pontoon or kick boat, it is steered with swim fins or small oars. The pontoon boat is easy to transport and allows anglers to fish and steer at the same time.

The type of boat most suitable to the Bow depends on the stretches of water to be floated. The Bow between its upper reaches and Calgary contains a wide variety of water types. Some stretches are very slow and calm, and others are dangerous and even impassable because of white water and numerous sweepers. The character of the water also varies widely within short stretches of river. Though there are sections of the upper river suitable for floating, anglers are advised to be absolutely certain of the nature of the water between the put-in and takeout points. The upper Bow is best floated in a McKenzie driftboat or a rugged, full-size inflatable.

Below Calgary the river has a gentle nature, with no rapids of consequence, but floaters approaching Carseland must heed signs and buoys warning not to take a boat or canoe over the irrigation weir. Fly-fishers are advised to consult local canoe clubs or the publications recommended in Chapter 1 for information about the navigability of the waters they desire to drift fish.

Anglers sometimes equip their boats with outboard motors to return from their float trips. This is not always satisfactory, however, especially during August and September, when low water levels sometimes render motors ineffective—much to the chagrin of boaters, who may be quite literally stuck down the river without a paddle. Fly-rodders who wish to use outboards are best advised to motor upstream the desired distance at the beginning of the trip and then drift down to their vehicle. This way they are at least certain they can return to their vehicle if there is a breakdown.

Rowing a Driftboat

With most activities there is an easy way and a hard way to get the job done. The easy way to row a boat in moving water is to use the current to help steer. The hard way is to fight the current. The best way to use the current is to position the boat in the water so the person at the oars is looking downstream and can see where the boat is going. Steering is accomplished by simply rowing the boat as if trying to move it upstream. That won't happen, but the boat will move toward one bank or the other, depending on which way the boat is pointing when the oarsman starts to row. For example, if the rower wants to move the boat nearer to the right bank, he simply turns the boat so the end of the boat behind him points slightly toward the right bank. If he then rows upstream, the boat will move diagonally downstream toward the right bank.

Beyond these basics there are subtleties to rowing a drifting boat that can only be learned by spending time at the oars. Capable oarsmen are a distinct advantage when drift fishing, and they deserve a good portion of the credit when fish are caught on the drift.

*Johnboats
and other
craft with
square sterns
(as shown in illus-
tration) should go
downriver stern first.
McKenzie River
driftboats are
designed to go
downriver bow
first. No matter
the style of boat,
the oarsman
faces down-
stream and
can see
where the
boat is
going.*

Fishing from a Drifting Boat

Fly-fishing from a drifting boat presents some interesting challenges. First of all it is imperative that the oarsman doesn't try to fish. It just doesn't work because success is partly a function of the oarsman's ability to keep the boat in an advantageous position for the caster. Most fishing partners take turns on the oars, often trading places each time a fish is caught. Other anglers use the 20–20 rule: one fishes for 20 minutes or until a 20-inch fish is landed before taking a turn at the oars. One day when my friends Neil Jennings and John Knoeck were fishing according to the rule, John landed a big trout, making it his turn to row. They traded seats and Neil flopped a streamer over the side of the boat just as John pushed off from the bank. A big rainbow took the fly, and before anybody could do anything it jumped and landed right on the net in the bottom of the boat. John picked up the netted fish, held it up to Neil and said, "Nice fish. Your turn to row."

Most of the time the best way to fish from a boat is to work the banks, where fish often hold for shelter and relief from the current. The oarsman keeps the boat a comfortable casting distance from the best-looking bank (usually the outsides of bends), and the anglers cast to the holding water next to the bank. The fly must land within inches of the bank. I used to tell clients that a fly cast a foot from the bank might be close enough, but that three or four inches was better. This is not a hard and fast rule, yet it is a good starting point from which to try variations. You should bear in mind that the fish tend to move away from the banks in autumn, when the water level drops too low to provide adequate security. They also will move away from the banks on days when driftboat traffic is especially heavy.

The oarsman should change rowing tactics according to the fishing method being used. When anglers are casting streamers, for example, the rower should slow the boat so the fly swings around downstream of the boat during the retrieve. If dry flies are being used, the oarsman should allow the boat to drift at the same speed as the current or slow it very slightly to help give the fly a long, drag-free drift. If nymphs are being cast the boat should usually be closer to the bank because nymphs must be fished with a relatively short line. Of course, if a particularly good lie is spotted, the oarsman should row like mad straight upstream to slow or even stop the boat so anglers can get several casts into it.

Drift fishing requires that you watch ahead and identify your target before you get to it. It is usually best to angle the casts slightly downstream—in other words to hit the spot before the boat is directly across from it. If you're casting a dry fly, try to have it land right on the current seam at the point where moving water meets still water near the bank. Let the fly drift naturally, making upstream mends as necessary to ensure a drag-free drift. If you're using a streamer the usual method is to cast the fly close to the bank beyond the current seam. Vary the retrieve to discover what works best. The objective is to make the fly swim across the seam, getting the attention of fish. Occasional upstream mends can help.

An effective if somewhat unconventional method of fishing streamers from a drifting boat has been developed over the years by George McBride and Eric Grinnell. The oarsman slows the boat as it drifts along the bank, and the angler casts a fast sink-tip line up and across to the top of a good run or seam in the current. The angler makes a couple of upstream mends to slow the fly and allow it to sink, and then retrieves very slowly, trying simply to stay in touch with the fly and give it occasional twitches as it drifts down the run. The fly eventually passes the boat, and when the line straightens out below, the angler casts again. This method keeps the streamer swimming deeply along the current seam.

When you cast from a drifting boat you quickly learn that you usually get only one shot at each prime spot before drifting past it. There is always a temptation to reach back upstream for one more cast at a particularly juicy lie, but it rarely works. If the fly is a streamer it races downstream faster than the current and faster than most fish want to chase. If a dry fly is cast it immediately starts to drag.

When I was guiding I used to try to prepare anglers for particularly good spots that we were approaching, but I gave it up as a jinx. A couple of casts before we'd get there, I'd say, "There's a real nice lie coming up by this fallen tree. Make sure to get a good cast in there." Immediately and invariably one guy would hook himself in the back while the other would fire his fly right into the fallen tree, or their lines would become hopelessly entangled.

When you cast from a drifting boat for the first time you can get confused because the frame of reference is moving, and you try to relate everything to the drifting boat. For example, when a fish rises between the boat and the bank, you tend to cast repeatedly toward the rise form, which is drifting downstream with the boat. You don't realize that the fish is still back there where it rose—some distance upstream. You must take your point of reference from the bank, not the moving boat.

If two anglers are casting from a boat they must cast parallel to each other to avoid tangles. The one in the downstream seat must be especially careful not to cast so far upstream that his line will cross his partner's. This is called poaching and usually elicits severe verbal abuse from the other angler.

Small fish that can be played and landed quickly may be released easily from the boat by just twisting the hook out of their mouths. Larger fish that require careful playing to land, however, should not be released from a moving boat. It is awkward at best and often not conducive to successful resuscitation of the fish. The oarsman should pull the boat into the bank before the fish is landed, and the fish should be thoroughly revived in quiet water in the usual manner. Pulling the boat in also will allow you to fish the rest of the good water you would otherwise drift through while playing a trout.

RIVER ETIQUETTE

Given the heavy use and wide range of recreational activities taking place on the Bow, it is inevitable, I suppose, that misunderstandings occur between users. Over the years I have been involved in my share of these and have come to believe that very few are of an intentional nature. Most stem from a lack of understanding of other people's use of the river.

Many problems occur between fly-fishers and canoeists, especially between Calgary and Carseland, where the gentle nature of the river appeals to families, particularly on weekends. These folks are typically enjoying the beauty of the river valley and for the most part wouldn't antagonize a flea, but their curiosity sometimes gets them in trouble.

Canoeists often find it fascinating to watch someone casting a fly. Frequently they want to get a closer look, and they paddle quietly right behind a drifting boat. The anglers and oarsman in the drifting boat are invariably directing their attention and their casting toward the bank, and are completely unaware of the canoe's presence. At some point a back cast whistles past a canoeist's ear, or worse yet, past little Johnny's ear, and Dad, who interprets this as a blatantly aggressive act, or at least extreme carelessness, hollers in a haughty voice, "Hey, watch where you're throwin' that thing!" The startled fly casters, of course, had been doing precisely that. I don't understand how someone can watch a fly-fisher cast for 10 minutes and then paddle over right behind him and still be surprised when a back cast comes near his head.

Another problem resulting from a lack of understanding can occur when boats or canoes pass too close to anglers on the bank. The average citizen who knows nothing about fish doesn't realize that trout are easily frightened and that once they're frightened they can't be caught. It aggravates anglers casting to rising fish when a boat drifts by within 15 feet of them. Putting fish down is bad enough, but insult is added to injury when the boater innocently asks, "How's fishin'?" A friend of mine was once asked by a romantic couple in a canoe if he would raise the tip of his rod a bit so they could get by. The rest of the river was between the canoe and the far bank, but for some mysterious reason they had to paddle within three feet of the angler.

The best approach to avoid conflict, of course, is to treat other users as you would wish to be treated if your positions were reversed. Anglers should gently inform nonanglers of the nature of their sport and explain how easily trout may be frightened. Education will greatly reduce misunderstandings on the river.

The two types of anglers on the Bow—those on foot and those

in boats—also run afoul of each other from time to time. Observing a few simple rules of etiquette will ensure harmony.

1 When a driftboat encounters a walking angler, the walking angler has the right of way. The driftboat should pull well around, giving the fly-fisher plenty of undisturbed water to fish.

2 When a walking angler encounters a stationary one, the walker should circle around, giving the other lots of water to fish.

3 When anglers encounter each other going in opposite directions, the one progressing upstream has the right of way.

4 When a driftboat wants to overtake a slower-moving boat, it should pull across to drift the other side of the river rather than passing like a car on a freeway and cutting in front.

5 Anglers drifting the river should not sneak a cast into other anglers' water as they go by, even if the other party is not casting at the moment.

6 Anglers in driftboats who encounter a parked boat or wading anglers in a tight spot should talk to them to find out how they'd prefer to be passed.

It's generally advisable, at least on the Bow below Calgary, to avoid floating small side channels. If you do you may quite suddenly come upon unseen wading anglers and have no choice but to drift right through the water they're trying to fish. These smaller channels should be fished on foot.

In addition, as the river gets busier, some etiquette at the boat ramps is in order. The requirement is simple: spend as little time as possible on the ramp and in the parking area with your boat and vehicle. Don't keep other people waiting while you check your blood knots, clean your fly line or tell fishing stories.

Conflicts also occasionally occur between anglers and private landowners. The onus is on the angler to be aware of the trespass regulations. In Alberta, lakes and streams, with a few rare exceptions, are designated as Crown land below the normal high-water mark, which is usually defined as the line of permanent growth of nonaquatic vegetation. An angler or recreational user who gains access to the water without trespassing and who stays below the high-water mark is generally considered to be abiding by the law. Nevertheless my personal approach, and the one I heartily recommend to visiting anglers, is to talk to the landowner if there is a house adjacent to the water you intend to fish.

PLANNING A TRIP

The Bow is not a river to approach unprepared. My advice to fly-rodders planning a trip to fish the Bow is to take care of as many details as possible before leaving home. If you are coming a long distance to fish a short time I strongly recommend you hire an experienced guide. They cost some money for a day's fishing, but you'll be as assured as possible of fishing the right water with the right tackle at the right time, and it seems to me those kinds of assurances are worth some money.

If you decide to hire a guide, you will be faced with a large pool to choose from. If possible ask advice from someone who has fished the Bow with a guide and get recommendations. Failing that, contact several outfitters yourself, but avoid the temptation to make a selection based solely on price. The best approach is to ask for references.

On the Bow, as elsewhere, the best guides will be booked up early, so make your plans as far in advance as possible. Many steady clients don't want to lose their guides and simply book their next year's visit before returning home.

When you book a trip with an outfitter, be sure to tell him your fishing preferences, your expectations, the extent of your fishing experience and any physical limitations you have. Once, I nearly killed an angler I was guiding because he waited until the end of a strenuous day to tell me he'd had a mild heart attack just a few weeks prior to his trip.

If you plan a trip to the Bow but can't afford the services of a guide, you will be wise to solicit information from local organizations such as the Calgary Hook and Hackle Club or the Trout Unlimited chapters in Calgary and Banff. You also can make contact with one of Calgary's or Banff's sporting goods stores or tackle shops to get additional information on fishing the river.

6

The Upper Bow River

Headwaters to Bearspaw Dam

THE UPPER BOW RIVER is a fine trout stream that would be more highly regarded were it not overshadowed by the river's reputation downstream. If the city of Calgary and all it means to the Bow downstream didn't exist, we would spend much more time fishing the upper river—and we'd love it. The upper Bow is a big river with lots of braided side channels, and it amply satisfies both big-river and small-water anglers. Much of the upper Bow also stays open all winter thanks to numerous springs that enter the river directly and through some of the side channels.

The Bow in its extreme upper reaches above Lake Louise is very clear and cold, and is too pure to possess the nutrients essential to prolific aquatic insect life. As well, like nearly all high mountain streams, it is subject to severe scouring during spring runoff. This prevents the growth of the algae that are a fundamental link in the food chain of a good trout stream. Consequently the river's

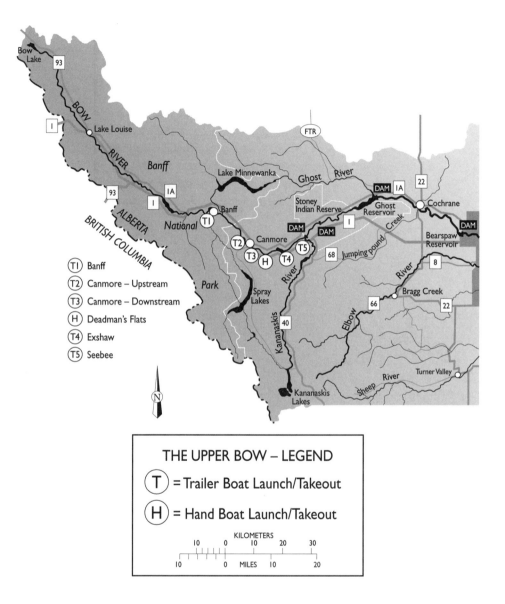

Bow Lake

93

BOW

1   Lake Louise

RIVER

Banff

93

ALBERTA

BRITISH COLUMBIA

1A

1

National   T1

FTR

Lake Minnewanka

Ghost River

Stoney
Indian Reserve

Banff

DAM

DAM   DAM

DAM   1A   22

Ghost
Reservoir

1

Cochrane

Creek

Bearspaw
Reservoir   DAM

68   Jumping pound   8

(T1) Banff

(T2) Canmore – Upstream

(T3) Canmore – Downstream

(H) Deadman's Flats

(T4) Exshaw

(T5) Seebee

Park

T2   Canmore

T3   H   T4   T5

River

Spray
Lakes

Kananaskis

40

Elbow   River

66

River

Bragg Creek

22

N

Kananaskis
Lakes

Sheep   River

Turner Valley

THE UPPER BOW – LEGEND

(T) = Trailer Boat Launch/Takeout

(H) = Hand Boat Launch/Takeout

KILOMETERS
10   0   10   20   30

10   0   MILES   10   20

overall quality as a trout fishery in its extreme upper portions is only fair though it carries a wide variety of fish: bull and brook trout, whitefish, cutthroats, rainbows and cutthroat–rainbow hybrids.

The fishing on the Bow improves somewhat near the town of Banff, where warm water and nutrients enter the river from both the town and the Cave and Basin Hot Springs. Brown trout make their appearance as the main attraction to anglers, and the numbers of whitefish and brook trout increase.

Serious fly-rodders prefer the river between Banff and the Seebee dam, where the river has the best combination of water-level stability and abundant aquatic insect life. The Bow here holds a decent population of brown trout, including some real hogs, and provides very good fishing to those who know the river well. The upper Bow, however, is not generous to casual anglers. Fish numbers are low enough that the uninitiated must usually cover a lot of water before finding fish. I consider local advice a necessity on this portion of the river, for its idiosyncrasies are not easily discovered.

The upper Bow is naturally relatively stable. Because its headwaters are within Banff National Park, where logging is not permitted, runoff is heavy but short, and the river does not easily become dirty following summer rainstorms. However, the Bow's natural stability is compromised somewhat below Banff by the presence of power dams on the Cascade River and at the Spray Lakes reservoir, which cause noticeable flow fluctuations.

Between Seebee and Cochrane the river is interrupted by more power dams that further increase the severity of flow fluctuations. Since fish cannot adapt well to frequent extreme changes in water level, the river is not as good a fishery here as it is above Seebee or below the Bearspaw dam, which regulates these fluctuations before the river flows through Calgary.

Below the Seebee dam the river flows through the Stoney Indian Reserve, where access is unreliable. The best fishing in this area is in Chief Hector Lake, where the Stoneys collect a daily fee from anglers who wish to try for the huge rainbows the lake produces. The waters of the Bearspaw reservoir also provide a good-quality rainbow trout fishery though access is somewhat difficult.

WINTER

Because so much of the upper Bow remains open through the winter, and because regulations allow year-round fishing upstream of the Highway 1 bridge below Canmore, a surprising amount of fly-fishing is available in what is normally considered the off-season. On the right day it is possible to ski at one of Banff's resorts in the morning and fish the upper Bow in the afternoon.

During the winter months it is wise to concentrate on streamers and smaller nymphs like Pheasant Tails and Bead-Head Princes in the slow parts of the river. The catch will likely be predominantly whitefish, which often seem more active than trout at this time of year.

SPRING

The pre-runoff months of April and May are a time of erratic and unpredictable weather near the mountains. If the weather is warm in early spring, the upper Bow River can sometimes reach 50°F (10°C) prior to runoff and can produce a short period of great fishing before the melting snow reaches the river. Other years the water doesn't get warm enough for the fish to become active until runoff has receded. Adding to the unpredictability is the fact that the spring water level in the river is generally very low and consequently more significantly influenced by releases from the hydro plants on the tributaries.

The main insect hatches in the spring are midges and Blue-Winged Olive mayflies. The midges are usually present in some numbers through most of the winter though fish don't typically begin rising to them until April. The Blue-Winged Olives arrive in late April, a few weeks after they start hatching on the river below Calgary. As on the lower river, the spring Olive hatch is often ignored by the trout.

Streamers provide the best fishing on the upper river prior to runoff. Patterns like the Woolly Bugger, in brown or purple, and Clouser Minnows are effective for good-sized brown trout. These streamers are usually fished on fast-sinking sink-tip fly lines. Nymphs like midge larva and Pheasant Tails also work for both whitefish and trout.

An April 1998 float I took on the upper Bow was representative of the pre-runoff season. Dan Bell, Dale Freschi and I launched Dan's wooden driftboat in Exshaw at the outlet of Lac Des Arcs and drifted to the Seebee dam. The weather was beautiful, and I moved a fish to a streamer on one of my first casts. On the whole though, it was clear we were pushing the season. Dan rowed the boat, Dale caught a few fish on streamers and I mostly took photographs. Two highlights of the day were our sighting of a rare Harlequin duck and the 19-inch (48-cm) brown that I caught a short distance above the takeout. But no one was disappointed, for on this part of the river, the spectacular setting is reason enough to be there.

Runoff usually begins in mid- to late May and lasts a couple of weeks. Though this puts a stop to conventional river fishing, a number of backwater areas between Banff and the Seebee dam fill with water from runoff. Good-sized browns often move into these backwaters since the silt sometimes settles out quickly and the water is clearer than in the main river. As the river drops and clears, the streamer fishing resumes, and fishing in general improves as the water temperature rises.

SUMMER

By late June prime dry-fly season has begun. The giant black stonefly called the Salmonfly hatches on the upper river, but in relatively sparse numbers. As well a brown stonefly from the *Perlodidae* family, in about #8 or 10, and a slightly larger golden stone begin to emerge from bouldery runs and logjams. Prior to and during the stonefly emergence, heavily weighted nymphs like the Gold-Ribbed Hare's Ear and the Yellow Stone in #6 or 8 will catch fish. After the adult insects have been around for a few days, the trout get used to seeing these large, clumsy bugs on the water, and the fishing becomes very good with Stimulator-type dry flies. Activity builds for several weeks as the big flies cause the brown trout to abandon some of their usual caution. Instead of examining potential food items with nervous skepticism, they move boldly out from under the logjams and undercut banks to slash and churn the water with inspiring vigor.

The stoneflies are joined in July by sparse hatches of Pale Morning Dun mayflies and evening hatches of caddisflies that on occasion can rival those downstream of Calgary in their intensity. In midsummer the larger Western Green Drake begins its emergence on the upper Bow. One of Alberta's largest mayflies, it hatches on lower elevation streams throughout the foothills in mid-June, but on the upper Bow it typically arrives in July and continues through August. The Green Drakes emerge in the afternoons, and the heaviest hatches occur on cloudy days.

By all accounts grasshopper patterns don't work nearly as well on the upper river as they do below Calgary, no doubt because the alpine nature of the upper river is less than prime grasshopper habitat.

AUTUMN

Early autumn on the upper Bow brings the return of the Blue-Winged Olive—the bookend hatch throughout Alberta—coupled with sporadic hatches of a #14 brown mayfly many anglers refer to as a Red Quill. The fishing holds up nicely through September, but in late autumn it can become disappointing when many of the bigger browns move into smaller tributaries, where they are protected, in preparation to spawn.

THE NATURE OF THE FISHERY

The main difference between the upper Bow and the rest of the river is the predominance of brown trout above Calgary and rainbows below. Browns love cover, particularly bankside cover, so successful anglers focus on deadfall, logjams and undercut banks. Browns also will hold along current seams, runs and drop-offs, but the best will almost always be in water with significant cover. Throughout the summer and autumn the upper Bow fishes best on cloudy or overcast days because browns are rarely active in bright, sunny conditions.

The size of the fish on the upper Bow won't average as high as below Calgary, but lengths of 18–22 inches (46–56 cm) and weights of over 5 pounds (2.25 kg) are not uncommon. Best of all, when all the pieces of the puzzle are in place on the upper Bow, dry-fly fishing becomes more than just a hopeful possibility—it becomes the most effective method to use.

Anglers who are consistently successful on the river below Calgary will hold their own on the upper river if they adjust their strategy and perhaps fish a little more quickly, covering more water than usual. As of this writing the fishing regulations within Banff National Park are under review and numerous changes are anticipated. Anglers must check regulations before fishing.

ACCESS

The upper Bow is quite accessible. The upper stretches above Lake Louise can be accessed from Highway 93. From the town of Banff downstream to Exshaw the river can be accessed from Highways 1 or 1A. In addition, reasonable foot access is available in the towns of Banff, Canmore and Exshaw, and at the Seebee dam. A short distance below Seebee the river enters the Stoney Indian Reserve, where access to the river becomes unreliable down to the town of Cochrane.

Driftboats can be launched from a number of places on the upper river, though conditions make their use impractical above the town of Banff. The first logical place to put a boat in the Bow is at the river's confluence with the Spray River at the west end of the town of Banff. Fifteen miles (24 km) and a full day's float from there is a takeout at the bridge near the golf course in the town of Canmore. The next possibility is a couple of miles downstream, beneath the Highway 1 bridge. Another 8 miles (13 km) down the river is a rough takeout below the Highway 1 bridge at the Dead Man's Flats campground. There is good water between the highway bridge and the campground, but since the stretch is heavily braided and prone to logjams it is best floated with a guide familiar with the route through the maze.

A 4-mile (6.5-km) float can be taken from Dead Man's Flats through Lac Des Arcs to the town of Exshaw at the east end of the lake. Anglers are advised, however, that the Exshaw area is known for the fierce winds that funnel through the valley even when wind is not a problem farther upriver. The final logical boat access on this part of the river is just above the Seebee dam, which can be reached via the access road between Highways 1 and 1A.

At the time of writing no commercial vehicle shuttle services are operating on the upper Bow, but this may change before long. For now, anglers must move their own vehicles prior to their trip or hire a taxi from Canmore.

UPPER BOW FLIES
Dry Flies

Month	Fly	Size	Imitates
April, May, June, July	Blue-Winged Olive Thorax	#16, 18	*Baetis* mayflies
June 15– July 30	Orange Stimulator	#2, 4	Salmonfly (stonefly)
June 25– September 5	Brown or Orange Stimulator	#8, 10	Medium Brown Stoneflies
June 25– August 30	Yellow Stimulator	#6, 8	Golden Stonefly
July 1– August 15	Olive Paradrake	#12	Small Western Green Drake mayfly

July 1– September 15	Green Elk Hair Caddis	#12–16	Caddisflies
July 1– September 15	Tan Elk Hair Caddis	#14–18	Caddisflies
July 10– August 15	Olive Paradrake	#8, 10	Western Green Drake mayfly
July 15– September 15	Pale Morning Dun Thorax	#14, 16	Pale Morning Dun mayflies
August 15– September 30	Red Quill	#14, 16	*Cinygmula* mayflies
August 20– October 10	Blue-Winged Olive Thorax	#14, 16	*Coloradensis* mayflies
September 15– October 15	Orange Stimulator	#8, 10	October caddisflies

Nymphs

Month	Fly	Size	Imitates
all season	Pheasant Tail	#10–14	Various mayflies and caddisflies
all season	Gold-Ribbed Hare's Ear	#8–12	Various mayflies and stoneflies
all season	Yellow Stone	#4–8	Golden Stonefly
all season	Bead-Head Prince	#10–14	Various mayflies and caddisflies

Streamers			
Month	Fly	Size	Imitates
all season	Clouser Minnow	#4, 6	Minnows
all season	Woolly Bugger (olive, purple or brown)	#4–8	Leeches and minnows
all season	Gander (grey or olive)	#4, 6	Sculpin minnows
all season	Bow River Bugger (olive or brown)	#4–8	Leeches and minnows

Note: Dates are approximate and will vary from year to year.

7

The Middle and Lower Bow River

Calgary to Grand Forks

THE CITY OF CALGARY lies in a geographical transition zone where the rolling parkland of the western Alberta foothills melts into the flat, seamless prairie that covers the eastern half of the province. As the river leaves the city, it flows through a wide valley dotted with stands of mature cottonwoods. The valley narrows and deepens as the river moves southeast, and as the land on top becomes flatter, the scenery at water level shifts from pleasantly pastoral to ruggedly spectacular. Sandstone cliffs rise straight up from the outsides of bends, and the scattered stands of cottonwoods are replaced by mixed deciduous and evergreen forest.

Simply because it is where I have spent the most time, I think of "my Bow River" as the portion downstream from Calgary to the Carseland weir, a stretch of about 50 miles (80 km). The river here is large but with a gentle disposition that has fascinated me and held my affection for nearly three decades. Although the city is not far

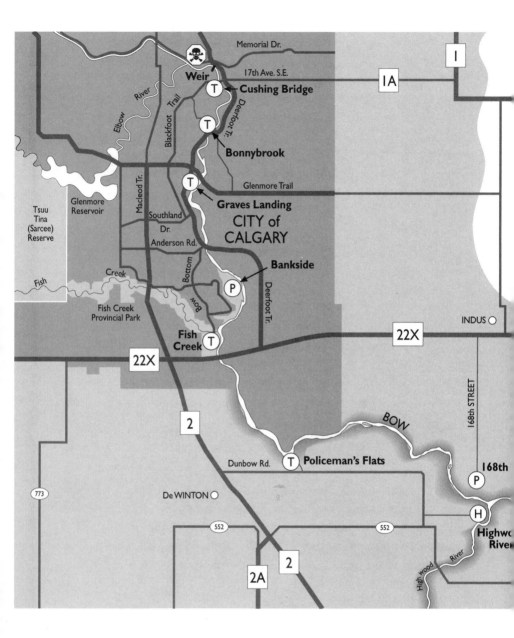

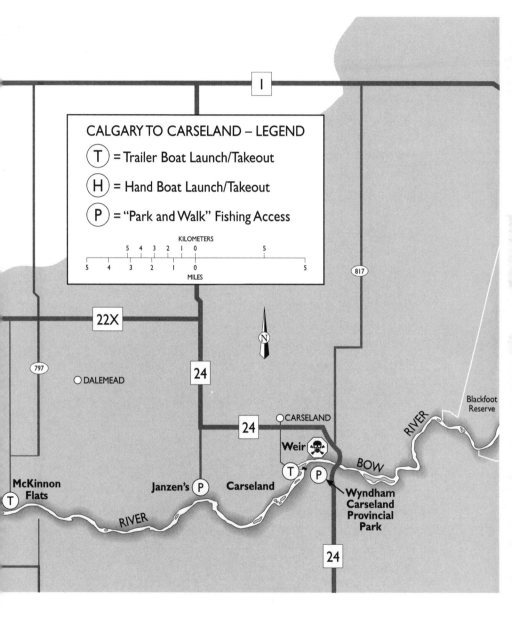

CALGARY TO CARSELAND – LEGEND

(T) = Trailer Boat Launch/Takeout

(H) = Hand Boat Launch/Takeout

(P) = "Park and Walk" Fishing Access

KILOMETERS

5 4 3 2 1 0   5

5 4 3 2 1 0   5

MILES

away, the valley remains for the most part wild. Few roads are visible from the water, and the most prominent signs of civilization's proximity are the rambling ranch houses that sit atop the river breaks, giving their owners a triply satisfying view of river, plains and mountains.

Though I can't deny that big trout are the main reason I frequent the middle Bow, I find the scenery appealing as well. The river valley is attractive and dramatic without being intimidating the way it often is in the mountains, and its abundant wildlife has become a big part of my Bow River experience. It makes me smile to myself to hear a cock pheasant squawk from the far bank or to watch a flock of mallards set their wings and drop into a side channel as I cast a dry fly. Such scenes make the fishing itself seem less important and yet more satisfying.

I've often noticed how an angler's opinion of a stream is influenced by the first visit there. For instance, many years ago on my first trip to one of the foothill streams west of Red Deer, I caught a 20-inch (51-cm) brown trout on my second cast. Needless to say this made a substantial impression. Even now, when I think of that stream, I remember the initiation rather than the span of five more years it took me to catch another fish this big there. So it was when I was first introduced to the Bow on October 10, 1970, a few miles downstream of McKinnon Flats. I rigged up quickly and caught two very nice rainbows while my companion, Jim Dixon, was stringing his rod. I was hooked—deeply—and my infatuation had begun.

I continued to fish the river a couple of times a year "from afar," while living in Edmonton and attending the University of Alberta. In the mid-1970s I began guiding fly-fishers on the Bow in the summers, and after a couple of years of moving back and forth between Edmonton and Calgary twice a year, my wife, Lynda, and I decided to stay in the southern city. I began to spend a lot of time on the river. The guiding business grew nicely, and by the early 1980s I was spending 60–100 days a year on this part of the river.

My experiences on the river have ranged from stimulating to meditative, from rewarding to frustrating. There have been revelations and disappointments, victories and defeats of an angling and an environmental kind. In the process my appreciation for the river has changed and, I think, matured. My feelings for the middle Bow River have grown from a initial infatuation with things that are obvious and spectacular to a deeper appreciation for that which is quiet and subtle. I must confess to holding this part of this river more dear than any place on Earth.

THE BOW ABOVE CARSELAND

A universal, unwritten law of trout fishing holds that there are places where you can catch *a lot* of small fish and places where you can catch *a few* large fish. It is generally agreed there are very few places where you can catch *a lot* of large fish. But the Bow between Calgary and Carseland is one of those special places. Most experienced Bow River fly-rodders catch good numbers of fish that average around 16 inches (41 cm) in length, allowing for the usual angler's hyperbole. Fish that would be the talk of the tackle shops on other streams are commonplace on the Bow.

The middle Bow's special status was driven home to me on an early trip to Montana. The owner of a famous flyshop suggested I try a certain stretch of the Madison River because someone had caught a 19-incher (48 cm) there two weeks before. This puzzled me because I knew that it wouldn't have been more than 20 minutes since somebody back home on the Bow had caught a comparable fish. Nineteen to 22-inch (48–56-cm) fish are daily occurrences on the middle Bow, and given normal conditions a veteran Bow River angler will consider things a little slow if he hooks fewer than 10–15 good-sized fish in a day. If a fish is to cause a stir among local anglers, it must be substantially larger than 24 inches (61 cm). There are streams where more trout, on average, may be caught in a day, but the Bow certainly isn't a one-lunker-a-day fishing hole.

The size of fish in the middle Bow has held up well over the years. Records I kept during one season of guiding many years ago indicate that 58 percent of the fish caught by clients were over 15 inches (38 cm) long and 23 percent were over 18 inches (46 cm). In contrast just 12 percent were under 12 inches (30 cm). Today fly-fishers continue to catch more fish over 20 inches (51 cm) than under 12 inches (30 cm). Visiting anglers shouldn't expect to do as well as experienced locals, but versatile fly-rodders who have some experience on big rivers and spend some time on the Bow will do all right. A large percentage of them will catch the biggest fish of their lives on the Bow. Accustomed to having to get as far away from civilization as possible to find good fishing, they are constantly amazed that large fish in large numbers can be caught within minutes of a metropolitan center.

The middle Bow is at its best when the large fish feed at the surface. A corollary of the universal, unwritten law of trout fishing states that when you finally find a stream with some big fish in it, you can bet they won't be surface feeders. But the Bow often breaks this rule, too.

Years ago I guided a pair of anglers from Wisconsin. Larry Trotter was an experienced fly-fisher and frequent visitor to the river. Tom Hoffmaster was just taking up the sport and was being initiated on the Bow. The fishing was fine, but Tom didn't realize he was being spoiled by the Bow, which had provided us with seemingly unlimited numbers of large, rising fish. At lunch one day, he said to Larry, "I like this. Why don't we do this in Wisconsin some time?" Larry laughed and said, "Because we can't. There isn't anyplace else in the world where we can do what we've been doing this morning." Though finding rising fish on the Bow is more difficult today than it was when I guided Larry and Tom, thousands of large fish are still caught each season on dry flies.

Perhaps the best summary of the way experienced fly-fishers regard the middle Bow is found in a letter I received from a Pennsylvania friend. Jim Gilson is a man possessed by fly-fishing, and his affliction has taken him around the world to sample the best. Upon returning home from his sixth annual visit to the Bow, he wrote me a letter:

> *I had some fine fishing on England's chalkstreams and limited success in Montana, but the Bow has set the standards by which all other trout experiences must be judged. It is imperative that friends*

*of the Bow do all they can to protect such an irreplaceable resource.
This is not just another blue ribbon trout stream we are dealing
with. The Bow is the finest trout river in the world!*

WINTER ON THE BOW ABOVE CARSELAND

If you were to ask hard-core Bow River anglers why they fish
in winter, you'd likely find them trying to deflect the query with
a clever, offhand remark. "It sure beats not fishing," they might say.
But soon they'd admit that winter or summer they simply have to
feed their habit. While many fly-fishers pack tackle away once the
snow comes, there is a surprisingly large group of Calgary anglers
who leave it in their cars during the winter months. They simply
wait for one of our Chinook winds to curl over the Rockies
toward Calgary, and then they head for the river. *Chinook* is an
Indian word meaning "snow eater," which is exactly what these
warm winds often do when they raise the temperature 40–50°F
(8–10°C) overnight. Frequent Chinooks coupled with several miles
of open river below the city provide some surprisingly good winter fishing conditions.

Although there is a strong element of novelty in wading a
stream and catching trout with a fly in January, most Alberta anglers,
if pressed, would agree that winter fishing appeals for reasons other
than just a chance to catch fish. The river is very beautiful in winter, and after an absence of a couple of months, the reunion is like
dropping in on an old friend. I find it somehow reassuring to see
that the river is alive and well.

The fishing in winter, of course, is different from summer. In
winter the fish gather in the big pools, where the water slows and
deepens. This, combined with water temperatures just above freezing, demands fishing with sinking flies and often sinking lines. The
technique can be summarized by the words *slow and deep.* Fish in
this cold water will be on the bottom and simply will not move far
to eat something. This puts the onus on you to get the fly as near
the fish as possible.

A common winter rig includes a high-density sinking line, a

very short leader and a leech or Woolly Bugger in #6 or 8. The cast is normally made across the current, and the fly is allowed to swing on a tight line downstream. A slow retrieve is often used after the swing is complete, and you proceed downstream through the pool, steelhead-style.

Conventional nymphing with a floating line and strike indicator also will take fish in winter. The best flies are the San Juan Worm and nymphs like the Gold-Ribbed Hare's Ear or Prince, which also must be fished very deeply.

The strike of a winter trout is very gentle. Fly-rodders waiting for the solid thump they feel in summer may be completely unaware that a fish has taken the fly and may miss most of the strikes they get. I have often felt silly responding to what I thought was an imaginary hesitation in the fly's drift only to find the fly attached to a trout.

On the Bow River just below Calgary even winter dry-fly fishing is an occasional possibility. Midges hatch through most of the winter but are nearly always ignored by the fish until a spell of warm weather arrives and some trout and whitefish will begin to rise.

When fishing the river in winter, you must be aware of some unusual hazards. One is the danger of drifting ice floes, which can be anywhere from platter- to piano-sized. If you're directing your attention downstream, you'll be unaware of the danger bearing down silently on you from behind. Check over your shoulder once in a while to avoid being knocked off your feet. Equally dangerous are shelves of ice extending for some distance from the riverbanks. Before walking out on the ice, you should ensure that it's thick enough to support you or that shallow water is beneath it.

Winter fly-fishing places a premium on companionship with other anglers. For one thing, the near-freezing water will prompt you to take more frequent warm-up breaks. For another, you'll be safer. Falling in will get some laughs from your fishing partners in July, but getting wet in January or February will be anything but funny.

It goes without saying that clothing appropriate to the weath-

er is an essential when fishing in the winter. Because of their insu-
lating qualities, neoprene waders are popular with winter fly-fishers. Gloves with the fingertips removed to allow manipulation of
the fly line also are essential gear.

The portion of the middle Bow open during winter appeals to
me for more than fishing. In recent years I've enjoyed spending a
few days each winter duck hunting. Many ducks, mostly mallards
(and for some reason mostly drakes), are found on the river long
after the vast majority of migratory birds have left for the warm
South. There is something almost primitive about forsaking the
comforts of home to slog through the snow and freezing cold in
the early morning. I guess the appeal is in the fact that the
rewards—material or mental—are very definitely earned. Mostly,
though, the duck hunting, like the fishing that goes before and after
it, is simply another good excuse to be on the river.

SPRING ON THE BOW ABOVE CARSELAND

Spring in Alberta is a teasing, agonizing time of year for anglers.
Although cabin fever may have reached epidemic levels, many of
Alberta's foothill and mountain streams are feeling the effects of a
cold winter until as much as a month after the weather has
warmed. Their fish are sluggish and disinterested, apparently of the
opinion that it is not worth the effort to acknowledge spring. We
go fishing, yes, but only because our instincts tell us it is time and
because the regulations say we may. Fishing on most streams during
the pre-runoff period hovers a little to one side or the other of
poor.

Fortunately, because of its distance from the mountains and its
lower elevation, the Bow in and below Calgary reaches decent fishing condition before many of the smaller trout streams farther west.
For many years the Bow below Calgary was closed to fishing in
April and May, and it used to drive Calgary anglers crazy to watch
the river during this pre-runoff time, knowing it was the only
stream around in prime fishing condition. We used to wait anx-
iously for the reopening of the river on June 1. Some years the fish-

ing was very good in early June, but other times runoff and season opening would occur almost simultaneously, and our torment would be extended a few more weeks.

Since 1988, however, the Bow River between Calgary and Carseland has been open to catch-and-release angling during the usual pre-runoff period of April and May. If spring arrives early and eager, the river warms up nicely, and the fish move out of their wintering pools to supply quite good fishing by mid-April. Action is largely confined to brown trout because many of the mature rainbows are away spawning in the Highwood system. Other years, when the spring weather is cool and rainy, the water temperature remains low and winter conditions prevail much longer.

Streamers and Nymphs

When the water temperature approaches 50°F (10°C) the fish begin to behave like summer trout. They spread themselves throughout the river and establish lies in depressions, in riffles, in deep, churning runs and in quiet water along the banks. The most reliable way to catch them at this time is on streamers and nymphs. I use the same techniques in spring that I do the rest of the year, but because the water is very low and very clear during the pre-runoff period, I use somewhat smaller flies than I might during the peak of summer. Good streamers for the pre-runoff period are the Bow River Bugger and Clouser Minnow in #6 and 8. If I'm wading and fishing I typically prefer a sink-tip line, but if I'm floating the river I find a floating line adequate.

Nymph fishers won't stray too far from proven patterns like the San Juan Worm, Gold-Ribbed Hare's Ear and Prince Nymph until the small Blue-Winged Olive mayflies begin to hatch in April. Then they turn to the Pheasant Tail Nymph in #14 or 16 as a good match. Blue-Winged Olives emerge from riffles in the afternoons, and if you see them hatching in numbers but no fish feeding on the surface, it's a good bet they are working on the nymphs in a riffle somewhere.

In May the fish begin to respond to golden stonefly nymphs in

#4 or 6. These insects begin to get active before they migrate to the banks to emerge, and a Brooks Yellow Stone or Kauffmann Golden Stone will usually attract some action.

Dry Flies

April and May on the middle Bow are almost always a time of heavy hatches but only occasionally a time when fish feed heavily on the hatches. The first important insect of spring is the little Blue-Winged Olive mayfly from the *Baetis* genus. It's a very prolific insect that hatches best on cloudy afternoons. In my experience it's an insect that the fish are reluctant to feed on in the spring—at least at the surface. Joe Cunningham and I fished this hatch one May afternoon a number of years ago when the surface of the water was fuzzy with the little mayflies. We walked about a mile of river to find exactly two fish rising. They were big browns and our search was certainly worth the effort, but it was puzzling why the fish were so reluctant to feed. My only theory is that the Blue-Winged Olives arrive at a time when the water is still a little colder than ideal for dry-fly fishing. When you do find fish eating Blue-Winged Olives, a Blue-Winged Olive Thorax in #18 or an Olive Floating Nymph in #16 will usually entice them. Strangely, when these same insects hatch again in the fall, the fish are much more likely to rise to them. I've added this phenomenon to my growing list of Bow River mysteries.

Caddisflies and the Western March Brown mayfly also begin to hatch during this pre-runoff period, and they sometimes produce very nice dry-fly fishing. The caddisflies emerge in May (so it's sometimes called the Mother's Day Hatch) on bright, sunny days. When the hatch gets rolling the fish usually respond to an Elk Hair Caddis or LaFontaine Emergent Sparkle Pupa in #14.

Once dry-fly fishing on the Bow has been kick-started by the caddisflies, the fish also will take Western March Browns. The March Brown is a good-sized bug—about #14—with a dark grey-brown color that is matched nicely by a Red Quill or March Brown dry.

The best dry-fly fishing I've had in the pre-runoff period was during a hatch of March Browns. Several years ago at the end of May, Russ Webb, fly-fishing writer Doug Swisher and I began a day with streamers and nymphs, but the program was soon interrupted by March Browns and rising trout. For a few hours there seemed to be fish feeding in every flat and tailout between Policeman's and McKinnon flats.

Though the pre-runoff period can produce some very fine fishing, it's a crapshoot whether the caddisflies and March Browns hatch before the runoff. During a warm spring the bugs begin hatching in mid-May to provide a couple of weeks of great fishing. Other years the weather is cool and runoff arrives first, so the insect activity is wasted on dirty water. In some years the hatch and runoff occur simultaneously, and as in baseball a tie goes to the runoff.

The intensity of runoff on the Bow River below Calgary is difficult to predict. Not only is the river subject to all the natural influences of winter snowpack, spring rain and spring temperatures, but it is also affected by the four dams between its source and Calgary. If water levels in the impoundments are low, mountain runoff, which starts with warm temperatures or rain in the high country, may be held back to fill the reservoirs. Under these circumstances there will likely be little or no runoff below Calgary. But if the reservoirs are nearly full, or if the winter snowpack is especially heavy, the water will be released, and levels will rise below the city as well.

Runoff usually reaches Calgary within a few days of June 1 and can be anything from a slight increase in volume and a stain in color lasting but a few days to an all-out brown surge that keeps the river unfishable for three weeks or more. During a heavy runoff the river takes on a decidedly robust personality. The normal flow in mid-summer is about 3,300 cubic feet (96 m^3) per second, but in a heavy runoff it will rise to about 10,000 cubic feet (291 m^3) per second. All kinds of stuff is carried by the river then, from plant debris picked up on the banks to whole trees to occasional dead livestock. One of the heaviest runoffs in recent memory occurred in 1995, when runoff coincided with a storm that dropped 4–6 inches (10–15 cm) of rain in 24 hours. Major flooding redesigned many of southern Alberta's trout streams. Since the runoff period can be a somewhat uncertain time for fishing, most guides and outfitters don't book any clients from out of province until near the end of the June.

Some of the best fishing of the year takes place as the river is receding from a normal runoff. A fact not widely known is that the river can fish very well when it is still somewhat swollen and carrying some color from snowmelt. I consider the river to be unfishable when it is an opaque grey-brown color, but when it takes on a foggy green hue and you can see into it 18 inches (46 cm) or more, it is ready to be fished.

SUMMER ON THE BOW ABOVE CARSELAND

Each summer a magical event happens on the Bow below Calgary, and its occurrence pleases me each time I witness it. As the water warms and stabilizes, the river begins its annual transformation from freestone river to giant spring creek. The water drops and clears to a fishable condition sometime between the middle and the end of June, weed growth appears on the bottom and before our eyes a new entity is born. A choppy run that required a high-density line and enormous flies a couple of weeks earlier may by mid-July present anglers with large trout surface feeding in flat, knee-deep water. This is the Bow River that I know and love best.

Fly-fishing is typically never better than during the second week of July, when Calgary comes apart at the seams as the Calgary Stampede draws would-be cowboys from all over the world to its carnival and real cowboys to its rodeo. There is a festive atmosphere on the river, too, for this is definitely the wildest time of the season. Everything seems to be happening at once. Streamer and nymph fishing are at their best as the hungry rainbows return from their spawning journey. Pale Morning Duns are on the water from late morning to early evening, followed by the nightly caddis attack. It's all a person can do to hold up his end and try to take it all in. And if that's not enough, the sun doesn't set until around 10:00 P.M. at this time of year, and the caddis activity lasts well into the night. Many local anglers don't even start to fish until about 9:00 P.M. This way they can return home from work, have a leisurely dinner with the family, put the kids to bed and then go fishing for a few hours. What better way to end a day?

Streamers

Though streamers are perhaps most effective as the river is clearing after runoff, they remain a good choice throughout the summer. Early summer streamer anglers prefer very fast sinking or sink-tip fly lines coupled with short leaders—much the same as the tackle used in winter. But when the water is high and still carries some color, flies as big as #2 and 4 are needed to get the attention of fish. The fly patterns chosen will depend on the latest fads and preferences (of the fly-fishers, that is). A few years ago the Marabou Leech, Marabou Dace and Spuddler patterns were hot. Then it was the Woolly Bugger and Zonker, and more recently it has been the Bow River Bugger, the Gander and the Clouser Minnow.

The fish at this time of year often hold very close to the banks, where they get relief from the strong current, making early summer the best time of year for "pounding the banks" from a driftboat. Many anglers load their 7- or 8-weight rods with fast-sink tips and lead-eyed buggers and embark on a "power float," say from the Highway 22X bridge to McKinnon Flats with no plans to stop except to land big fish. The only downside to this trip is the elbow pain you feel the next day.

In contrast to many of the fine rivers in the western United States where big brown trout are taken most frequently in the autumn, the middle Bow, in my experience, offers more big browns in early summer than any other time of year. I'm uncertain of the reason, but perhaps it is because some of the large rainbows have not yet returned to the Bow from their spawning run into the Highwood River system. This shouldn't make the browns easier to

dent early in the season. If I am
ish the water between the Glen-
:idges with big streamers as the
d- to late June.
he water has usually receded to its
e to produce but with less regular-
the fish become wary of streamers
ddening habit of chasing them but
itching to a smaller fly helps. Some-
ner the best times to fish streamers
f early morning or late evening and

Nymphs

Both streamer and dry-fly fishing can be spectacular on the middle Bow in summer, but when they aren't, versatile fly-rodders reach for their box of nymphs. Nymphs have in fact become the most reliable way to take fish on the Bow below Calgary. This is a bold statement, but it has become increasingly true as the river has been fished more heavily.

Nymphs can be fished in a variety of places, but through the summer I focus my attention on broken, choppy water, deflections along the banks, riffles leading into pools, and side channels.

Many anglers rig two nymphs at a time, and day in and day out the best combination is the San Juan Worm and something else. The something else can be a Yellow Stone Nymph, a Bead-Head Prince, a Gold-Ribbed Hare's Ear or a caddis larva. In the early part of summer, when the water is still a little high and discolored from runoff, my favorite something else is the Bitch Creek Nymph. This ridiculous-looking fly will scare fish later in touchy low-water conditions, but it gets eaten by them at this time of year.

In late summer the Bow also offers some opportunities for sight fishing, a technique best performed with two people. Once a fish is spotted one casts while the other does duty as fish watcher and coach, directing the casts, describing the fish's reaction and heckling. Pioneered on the Bow by guides like Mike Guinn and Dee Chatani, it is a most entertaining method of fly-fishing.

Dry Flies

Midseason on the middle Bow is signaled by the first appearance of the Pale Morning Dun mayfly, which entomologists tell me is *Ephemerella infrequens* or *Ephemerella inermis* or both. Some of the best dry-fly fishing the trout world has ever known has taken place on the Bow River during Pale Morning Dun hatches. The finest I ever experienced was one day in late June 1985, when Jim Gilson, Bill Conn and I hooked between 80 and 100 fish on dry flies. The fish averaged 17–18 inches (43–46 cm) long, and about a dozen of them were over 20 inches (51 cm).

The Pale Morning Duns generally appear in mid-June and typically hatch for a period of four to six weeks. Their emergence usually starts in late morning and often lasts through the rest of the day. The flies are about ⅜ inch (1 cm) long and have creamy olive bodies and pale dun-grey wings. Although the density of the hatch will vary from day to day, the Pale Morning Dun is a very reliable insect.

The Pale Morning Dun hatch can still be fished successfully with a standard Light Cahill in #16. Most anglers, though, prefer more specific Pale Morning Dun patterns such as the Pale Morning Dun Thorax or the Parachute Pale Morning Dun. A leader 9–12 feet (3–4 m) long and tapered to 4x or 5x is usually best.

A peculiarity of the Bow River's Pale Morning Dun hatch is the large number of freshly emerged duns that will be seen dead on the water. I don't know why there are so many cripples in this particular hatch, but at times they are far more abundant than live duns. The crippled duns can easily be mistaken for spinners because they float on the water with wings spent, and for practical purposes they can be thought of as spinners. In such conditions a Pale Morning Spinner dry fly imitates them well.

In the good old days it was common to find pods of 10–15 trout rising to Pale Morning Duns. Today it is more common to find a sneaky single sipping quietly in shallow water along a shady bank. My favorite part of the middle Bow River experience is find-ing a big fish rising greedily in 6–8 inches (15–20 cm) of water. I don't know if it's possible for a fish to be smug, but if it is, I know what it's thinking: *Nobody will ever suspect a big fish like me in this shallow water. There isn't a soul who knows I'm here.* These singles seem completely engrossed in what they're doing and are obviously enjoying themselves. I feel smug myself when I find one of them, for once hooked they explode with surprise, and because they can't go down, they just boil with panic for a moment in the shallows before streaking with bonefish speed toward deeper water.

While hatching insects are readily apparent on a river as large as the Bow, it can be difficult for inexperienced anglers to locate the feeding fish. They are very choosy about the type of water they favor, and they don't necessarily feed in all the places that might be expected. Bow River fish prefer to rise in water that is slow, rela-tively flat and almost always of wadeable depth. The preferred areas are usually along the banks, often on the side of the river opposite the heaviest current. They'll also rise on the insides of tight bends and along the banks at the tails of pools just above the point where the river gathers and breaks into a riffle.

Once rising fish have been located you must be able to discern the big fish from the small. When big trout are taking adult mayflies they rise much more deliberately than small ones and rarely make any noise or splash. I like to look for "snouts"—the heads of big fish that gently crease the surface when they take a insect. It is best not to be distracted by noisy, showy risers, for unless the fish are taking caddisflies, these probably aren't the fish you want.

When I'm snout hunting in Pale Morning Dun season, whether floating the river or on foot, I try to watch the water rather than cast blindly. If I were constantly casting I simply would not see some of the big fish feeding. Many times I have watched experienced fly-rodders walk right up on a big, sipping fish and put it down without ever seeing it. I'm certain that I have done the same dozens of times myself. In short no one posts signs saying, RISING FISH HERE! You must be prepared to hunt for them before fishing for them.

Once a prospect has been sighted the fishing is pretty much orthodox stuff. These trout have not yet developed the degree of leader shyness that some of their hard-fished American cousins have, so I prefer if possible to cast from a position downstream and slightly across from the fish. If they have been spotted from upstream, it is necessary to stay wide of their position when moving around them to avoid being detected.

The popular spring-creek method of fishing a dry fly from above so a trout sees the fly before the leader is rarely necessary on the middle Bow. In fact it can often be a poor approach. I recall one angler I guided who insisted on using the downstream dry-fly technique. I showed him a pod of large fish feeding voraciously, and in spite of my suggestions he insisted on getting above them and drifting his fly into the group from upstream. He caught a fish all right. One fish. A rainbow near the upstream end of the pod took his fly, turned and ran downstream through the rest of the school, and that was the end of their feeding. The angler, of course, was delighted that his downstream delivery had been successful, but I was tearing my hair out because I knew that by starting at the bottom and fishing up and across, he could have fished the pod for an hour or more and caught several.

To fish successfully with dry flies for rising trout on the Bow, you need to be able to cast accurately and manipulate the line and leader to get a perfectly drag-free float of the fly. During a plentiful hatch large trout don't move far from their lies to take a fly because they don't have to. They position themselves a few inches below the surface and consequently can only see a lane a few inches wide. Bow River fish have developed this habit to a degree that can frustrate anglers who haven't encountered it before. The fly nearly always must come within about 4 inches (10 cm) of the trout's nose to be taken. Pretty close is usually not close enough. Bow fish feeding on mayflies also will not tolerate drag on the fly. Though a dragging artificial will not always put the fish down, it will almost surely be ignored. Leaders with long tippets and a delivery that leaves slack in the leader are essential to consistent success. A modest representation of the insect delivered and fished properly will usually be taken, while a fly that is dragging or is out of the fish's feeding lane will be refused repeatedly, no matter how exact the imitation may be.

About the same time the Pale Morning Dun appears, another entrée is served up by the river. Caddisflies of various genera, including *Brachycentrus* and the free-living *Ryacophila,* emerge late in the evenings through midsummer. The flies range from about #12–18, and most are a dusty grey-brown color. They emerge in numbers that are hard to believe and get so thick at times that they become unpleasant. Bugs are everywhere—in your ears, inside your shirt, behind your glasses.

Favored caddis patterns on the middle Bow River are the Elk Hair Caddis and Gary LaFontaine's Emergent Sparkle Pupa. For improved visibility late in the evening, some anglers use a white-winged fly like the Trude with good results. And surprisingly, after dark, a black Elk Hair Caddis is often quite visible because it shows up well against the silver sheen on the water.

The caddis hatch generally brings greater numbers of fish to the surface than the mayfly hatches. Where Pale Morning Duns or Blue-Winged Olives bring large fish up in certain preferred places, strong caddis activity seems to make the entire river erupt with rising fish of all sizes. The fish also feed on these flies in a much wider variety of water, ranging from shallow riffles to medium-deep runs to slow flats.

When the fish are feeding on caddisflies, it is often difficult to determine the size of the fish because all sizes feed in the same slashing manner. The fish also move around a great deal, so casting to a rise form often becomes a visit to a trout's former address. My approach is to simply flail away in the dark and hope for the best.

When the trout are taking adult caddisflies laying eggs on the surface, the fishing is quite easy, and many different fly patterns prove effective. The "sudden inch" method of twitching the artificial just upstream of the trout can be devastating at such times. At other times, however, the fishing can be very frustrating, especially when it is difficult to distinguish whether the fish are taking adults or pupa. The rise of a fish taking an emerging pupa looks very similar to that of a fish taking an adult fly, and the thousands of flies in the air may convince you that the fish are eating adults when they are not. Sometimes there will be literally clouds of flies in the air but none on the surface of the water.

Another difficulty of fishing the caddis hatch arises when the fish begin to gently sip spent insects. The rise form looks just like the rise to a mayfly spinner and almost always occurs well after dark, making it difficult to see what's really happening on the surface of the water. Add to this the fact that certain species of caddis adults actually swim to the bottom to lay their eggs and the confusion is complete. You then may be faced with the possibilities of adults laying eggs on the surface, pupa emerging from the stream bottom, adults entering the water and swimming to the bottom to lay eggs, or spent adults on the surface.

Generally the key to sorting out the caddis hatch confusion is found in the rise form. If the fish are making a commotion they are likely taking emerging pupa or adults. If they are gently sipping they are probably taking spent caddis or are not feeding on caddis at all. In the latter instance they may be sipping mayfly spinners that snuck into the scene unnoticed.

One day in late July someone will whisper in the back corner of a Calgary flyshop, "I caught four fish on hoppers yesterday." Within hours similar whispers will be heard throughout the city. Grasshopper season, one of the most enjoyable times of year on the middle Bow, has arrived.

Hopper fishing is appealing because it catches large fish regularly and allows fly-rodders to use big dry flies, such as Stimulators and Letort Hoppers, that can be easily seen. Hopper imitations are extremely popular with anglers floating the river because they can be very effectively fished from a drifting boat. Anglers simply cast slightly downstream to the edge of the current along the bank, make an upstream mend and then watch the fly. When it moves away from the current edge or starts to drag, it is recast. The fly spends a lot of time on the water and can attract fish from some distance, even when they aren't actively rising.

Hoppers also are effective for wading fly-rodders. Choose a

section of river where there is moderate depth, current along a bank and hoppers nearby. Work your way upstream, concentrating on the water near the bank.

Bow River trout must not read fishing magazines, for they don't seem to know that they're supposed to take hoppers violently. Instead they usually take them in slow motion, starting their move toward the surface when the fly is still some distance away. I don't know if *you* can refrain from striking too soon when a 20-inch (51-cm) brown trout hangs at the surface waiting for your fly to drift the last two feet into its open mouth, but most of the time *I* can't.

Grasshopper fishing can run hot or cold from day to day, from hour to hour or even from one stretch of the river to another. Sometimes you can cover a couple of miles in a driftboat without any action and then in a quarter of a mile have half a dozen big fish take the fly.

About the same time the hoppers get active on the grassy edges and clay banks of the river, stoneflies are also abundant, as evidenced by the many empty shucks seen on rocks along the river's edge. Happily the flies we use to imitate grasshoppers and adult stoneflies are similar, and the fish can take them for either.

The only minor aggravation during the summer comes from the frequent evening thunderstorms that sometimes drop substantial rain. A heavy rainfall in the city will cause the river below the city to turn very muddy very quickly because storm sewers in older districts still drain directly into the river. Once the rain stops, however, the river clears again very soon. A brief, severe shower can cause the river to go from completely clear to completely muddy and back again in as little as 24–48 hours.

Two mayflies, the Trico and the Blue-Winged Olive, dominate the middle Bow's late summer hatch chart. The good news is that both hatches are prolific and long lasting. The bad news is that both insects are tiny. The *Tricorythodes* begins to hatch in early August and continues daily for six to eight weeks. The insect is unique for the short period of time it spends as an adult. Duns usually emerge through the night and molt into spinners the next morning—early in the day at the start of the hatch in August and progressively later throughout September. The spinners then gather in huge mating swarms that at times are dense enough to look like fog along the banks of the river. As the sun warms the air, the spinners swarm closer and closer to the water, finally dropping to the surface to lay their eggs and die when the air temperature reaches about 68°F (20°C).

When the spinners hit the water, they are available to the fish in the tens of thousands. The emerging duns can be important, too, particularly very late in the evening or on cold mornings, when the flies hatch but seem reluctant to molt and the duns tend to remain longer on the water.

Two factors make fishing the Trico hatch demanding. The first is the small size of the fly, which, for the Bow's Tricos, can be about #20 or as tiny as #24. The second is the number of flies on the water at once. Your imitation literally gets lost among all the naturals, and simple math indicates that chances for a strike are not good. This makes it doubly important to cast accurately and to keep the fly in front of the fish as much as possible.

Anglers must have some tricks up their sleeves if they are to fish the Trico hatch successfully. One is to fish a fly much larger than the actual Trico, which allows you to use a heavier tippet than you would need with a #20 or 22. I've had good luck at times with a #16 Adams and 4x tippet. Another option is to use a cheater pattern that uses a hook one or two sizes larger than what is suggested by the insect on the water but which keeps the dressing of the fly the correct size. For example, I often tie Trico Spinners with tails, body and wings in a #20 but do so on #16 hooks. It works well. Yet another alternative is to try a fly totally different from the natural to draw the attention of fish. Sometimes these work better than a "correct" imitation. The best example is a Red Flying Ant in #18. It is a bright red fly with a grey down wing and black hackle in the middle. It looks nothing like a Trico, but it either works very well or not at all, as fly-fishing logic would suggest. The trick was shown to me by Leigh Perkins of the Orvis Company, who suggested I avoid trying to figure out why it works when it does. I have taken his advice. When best tricks don't work and the fish want a

Trico Spinner of the right size and nothing else, you reach for your reading glasses to get the silly thing tied on, and then you throw the tiny bug in front of the trout, hoping you'll somehow know when it takes your fly from among all the naturals.

Through the 1980s the Tricos were a favorite hatch of Bow River trout, but a decade later they seemed to be increasingly ignored. Again I have no plausible theory to explain this change in behavior and no predictions about what the twenty-first century will bring. It won't surprise me, however, if the fish regain their taste for Tricos sometime in the future.

To complement the morning hatch of Tricos, there is usually an afternoon hatch of Blue-Winged Olives (a reprise of the first spring hatch), which begins in August and continues into September and October. These flies provide fishing similar to the Trico hatch, and some of the tricks I employ for the Tricos also work for this one. My favorite flies to imitate this insect are the Blue-Winged Olive Thorax or Adams, both in #18 or 20, and an Olive Floating Nymph in #16 or 18.

In recent years rising fish on the Bow are becoming more cautious. In some well-known dry-fly locations the fish have indeed become quite difficult to fool, so much so that guides sometimes bypass these places when they are out with less experienced anglers. But I often find myself seeking out these more difficult trout, for along with memories of fish I have caught are even fonder memories of those I couldn't catch. Perhaps it's another example of how, early in our outdoor lives, we are intrigued with the prospect of understanding something completely, and how, later on, after experience has taught us a few things, we become equally intrigued with the certainty that we never will.

AUTUMN ON THE BOW ABOVE CARSELAND

If July draws me to the river for the exciting fishing it offers, fall appeals for its contrasting change of pace. When an early frost draws red and yellow out of the cottonwoods and willows, when the sun stays low in the sky all day and the afternoon breeze carries the redolence of September, my attention is divided more evenly between what's in the river and what surrounds it. Back in spring I was filled with the exaggerated expectations that are the product of seven months of winter, and, rightly so, I fished myself silly to the end of summer. But with autumn comes the feeling that I should slow down, look around and fish in a more relaxed manner and at a more comfortable pace.

Dry Flies

Both the Trico and Blue-Winged Olive hatches continue well into September with the Blue-Winged Olive lasting the longest. I have had consistently good dry-fly fishing to the middle of October (and even into November some years) though the daily feeding period gets quite brief as the season wanes.

Blue-Winged Olives emerge heaviest on cool, overcast or drizzly days in September. Ironically the best fishing is often on days when most anglers stay home, but I know of no more reliable conditions for bringing big fish to the surface. So the borderline days when you're considering staying home are the days to hit the river. Pack your rain jacket, gloves and neoprene waders.

One such September day I floated a section of the middle Bow with Mike Gifford and Neil Jennings. Neil had to be back in Calgary about 3:00 P.M. for a meeting, so we arranged to leave his truck at a point halfway through the float. Fishing in the morning was spotty. The weather was cold, and the Tricos sputtered and didn't show up in fishable numbers. About 2:00 P.M. the Blue-Winged Olives began to emerge, and as we rowed Neil to his drop-off point, all three of us knew exactly what was going to happen. As Neil drove reluctantly away, Mike and I drifted around the corner, pulled the boat up on the gravel and spent two glorious hours working on big, rising fish. Amid our excitement we occasionally did stop to pity Neil, not just because he was missing the superb fishing, but because he had to endure the pain of *knowing* he was missing it.

A difficulty of fishing mayfly imitations on these overcast autumn days is the fact that the sky, the water and your fly all appear much the same dull grey color. In such conditions the Parachute Adams, with its beaconlike white wing, is a great fly to use.

The Trico and Blue-Winged Olive hatches have their ardent fans—usually people who have a high tolerance for punishment. I must admit to membership in this club, for I have come to accept the difficulty of fishing with tiny dry flies as part of the fun or perhaps even the source of the fun. Landing a big fish on a tiny dry fly is a memorable event, and the middle section of the Bow River is one of the best places in the world to take a 20-inch (51-cm) or bigger fish on a #20 or smaller fly.

Streamers and Nymphs

Casting sinking flies is more problematic in low-water autumns, when the aquatic weed growth is especially heavy, but the difficulty is manageable as long as the weeds remain attached to the river bottom. Such is not always the case on the middle Bow, however, since water levels constantly fluctuate very slightly. A tiny increase in level will cause large numbers of weeds to break loose and drift in the current. When this happens, they catch on lines, leaders and flies. Happily, if the water drops even an inch or two overnight, much of the weed will be deposited on the banks and will stay there until the water rises again.

Drifting weeds occasionally get so bad that fishing a standard streamer becomes almost impossible, so some anglers resort to flies tied with a monofilament weed guard. The weed guard probably costs some hookups by interfering with the hook point, but I find it beneficial in the long run because the fly spends more time unfouled by weeds. Another way to make streamers weedless is to simply tie them upside down so the wing itself deflects weeds past the hook point. Fly-fishers also can reduce the difficulties weeds pose by avoiding the outsides of bends, where the drifting weeds often collect.

In spite of the occasional difficulty, streamers remain effective through the latter half of the season. Often the need for extra fast-sinking or high-density fly lines is decreased because water levels are low and the fly must be kept near the surface to avoid the weeds. Guides on the Bow often have clients use unweighted streamers on floating lines when drift fishing in late season.

White Marabou streamers are favored in low-water conditions because they are highly visible to both fish and anglers. This is very entertaining sport because anglers see nearly all the strikes they get. Sometimes, when you're watching the white streamer work its way back toward the boat, it will disappear or suddenly jump sideways as a dark-bodied fish smashes the fly. You see it before you feel it. Many strikes produce vicious boils on the surface that excite even the coolest of anglers. Sometimes, too, you learn about the way fish take a streamer because you see them approaching for some distance. I recall fishing streamers in low water one day with sportscaster Curt Gowdy and Bow River guide Eric Grinnell. It seemed every trout in the river wanted our White Marabou Muddlers. Often several fish would chase the fly at the same time. Several times I intentionally cast the streamer into what I considered to be very poor, characterless water, only to have trout materialize from nowhere to slap at it.

Two anglers fishing from a drifting boat in late summer or autumn can pair a streamer with a hopper with good effects. I recommend that the angler in the downstream seat use a hopper to get the first opportunity at the banks while the second covers the same spot with a streamer. It is a good way to show the fish a couple of different choices.

Nymphs also continue to take fish throughout the autumn season. Because of the heavy weed growth in the fall, it is sometimes necessary to concentrate on the channels through the weeds or on areas of heavier broken water, where weeds don't grow as densely. The same patterns that work through spring and summer are good in the late season though I think it wise to fish with slightly smaller flies. Two favorite nymphs for September and October are the Prince Nymph and the Pheasant Tail in #14 or even 16.

Autumn brings to some people a sense of loss and nostalgia for the many things that are coming to an end, but I don't share their feeling. Autumn is my favorite time of the year, and I'd gladly trade

April and May for another October. To me this is the best part of nature's performance, the grand and triumphant spectacle of the turning of the seasons. On the middle Bow the yellow cottonwood leaves, some still in the trees and some carpeting the ground, the dark blue-green spruce and the deep autumn sky always conspire to make the river look deliciously alive.

On the clear, sunny days with the crisp mornings and evenings that are standard autumn fare in Alberta, I like to prowl the river in search of rising fish. I am more reflective at this time than earlier in the year, and I notice I am ambling toward a stretch of water that I would have wanted to run to in July. I stop and look for a minute at a spot that earlier held a real champion brown trout. As I wait for him to tell me he is still there, I puzzle over whether it was this summer or last that I caught him. I find rising fish farther along but decide they are not the ones I want today. There will be more upstream in a spot more rich in memories. As I move on I chuckle at how spoiled the Bow River has made me. I pass up sizeable trout that most fly-fishers only dream of simply because I prefer to fish another place on the river.

I arrive at the spot where a side channel leaves the main river, and I sit on a familiar fallen log to watch a minute. Before long I see a gentle dimple repeating itself near the far bank of the channel. I wade carefully toward it and lay out a few casts. Eventually the dimple happens at the end of my leader, and I raise the rod. The trout bolts at the feel of the hook and turns sharply downstream. The leader wraps around the thick weeds and the tippet snaps. I smile. In July I would have cursed.

Back at the fallen log I try to decide whether to replace the tippet and look for another fish or simply sit awhile before heading home. The frenzy of summer has been neutralized by the calm of autumn.

THE BOW BELOW CARSELAND

A few miles downstream of the town of Carseland, about 40 miles (64 km) from Calgary, the Bow River enters the Blackfoot

Indian Reserve. The river here flows through a lonely, magnificent prairie wilderness.

To anglers the real distinction between the river above and below Carseland—and it's a huge one—is the lack of fishing pressure below the town. Because of access difficulties and its distance from major population centers, the Bow here does not get a fraction of the angling traffic that occurs above Carseland. The fish are thus less inclined to be moody and reluctant to strike in the manner of those above Carseland. And though there's no solid scientific data to prove it, some anglers insist that the trout below Carseland are less plentiful but of larger average size than those above.

Streamers are the staple method on the Bow below Carseland, and it's a rare day when they don't work well. Nymphs also work well here though the river is noticeably slower and flatter and contains fewer sections of riffles and broken water, where nymphs are most easily fished. In late summer and autumn, dry flies, including caddisflies and grasshoppers, often work very well.

THE LOWER BOW RIVER

With one major exception—the absence of buffalo—the gentle valley of the Bow River between Bassano and the Grand Forks probably looks today much as it did when Jerry Potts first led the North-West Mounted Police into southern Alberta over a century ago. If you look you can still find the bones, teeth and skulls of the buffalo that lived in the valley for centuries before Chief Crowfoot's Blackfoot Nation and then Colonel Macleod arrived. This is short-grass prairie, a still largely uninhabited wilderness, where the dominant features are grass, sky and wind. The landscape may look drab but it's far from lifeless. A close look will reveal antelope, rattlesnakes, prickly-pear cactus and tiny, perfect wildflowers. Most of the changes made to this landscape by people over the last 100 years have been minor: the addition of a few fences, some oil wells, the occasional gravel road.

Irrigation withdrawals at Carseland and Bassano often divert more than half the water out of the Bow, and the result is that the river below Bassano becomes a small river in a big channel. The water is warm, slow moving and unattractive to anglers accustomed to the sparkling riffles and deep pools of the river in its upper and middle portions.

The lower river runs more than 100 miles (161 km) between the Bassano dam and the Grand Forks, but except for a popular spot immediately below the dam, less fishing takes place in this stretch of the river than in a single mile of the Bow between Calgary and Carseland. Trout are occasionally caught in the lower river, but by and large it is a warm-water fishery carrying pike, walleye and goldeye. Many eastern Alberta anglers enjoy these gamefish, but they can usually find more and bigger examples in the impoundments and lakes nearby. Additionally, the fishery of the lower Bow is unreliable because of unstable water conditions.

ACCESS

Access to the Bow in Calgary and down to Carseland has changed little in recent years. Good boat access is available in the city at the Cushing bridge on 17th Avenue, at Bonnybrook (Ogden Road bridge), at Graves Landing (Glenmore Trail bridge) and at Fish Creek (just upstream of the Highway 22X bridge). It's about 2 miles (3 km) from the Cushing bridge to Bonnybrook and another 2 miles (3 km) to Graves Landing. Graves to Fish Creek is 9.5 miles (15 km), which I consider a full day's drift, allowing for stops to fish on foot. There's some great water along this float, and it's a favorite of fly-rodders looking for big brown trout. Additional foot access to the river is available in Fish Creek Provincial Park, located in Calgary's south end.

Although these access points are entirely within the city, there is some distance between the angler and suburbia. Roads and buildings and the noise that attends them are apparent, but they don't press against the riverbanks. Because much of the land adjacent to the river is relatively undisturbed, wildlife is surprisingly abundant within the city limits.

Approved life jackets must be worn while boating or canoeing within Calgary's city limits, and you must be careful to avoid the dangerous weir located below Prince's Island, downstream of the Canadian National Railway bridge. Finally, fishing is prohibited within the Inglewood Bird Sanctuary, situated on the west bank of the river between Cushing and Bonnybrook.

Downstream of the city, boat access points are located at Policeman's Flats, which is about 5 miles (8 km) below the Highway 22x bridge on the south bank, and at McKinnon Flats, 15.5 miles (25 km) down from Policeman's Flats on the north bank. Below that is a boat access near Wyndham–Carseland Provincial Park, just above the Carseland weir on the north bank. The weir must be avoided when floating, but plenty of signs warn of its location.

Access also may be gained to the Highwood River about .5 miles (.8 km) above its confluence with the Bow. Here a canoe or light cartop boat can be put in the river for a float down to the Bow.

In addition to the boat launching sites there are two park-and-walk access points between the Highway 22x bridge and the Carseland weir. One is just above the mouth of the Highwood River on the north bank, and the other is about 9.5 miles (15 km) below McKinnon Flats and also on the north bank. Both provide a parking spot at the top of the river valley and require a hike down the steep embankment to the river.

Anglers will benefit from the excellent map produced by the Bow River Chapter of Trout Unlimited. The map shows access to the river between the Bearspaw dam and the Carseland weir and provides other useful information for anglers new to the river. It's available at most tackle shops in Calgary.

Other than the Carseland weir and the Highway 24 bridge a mile or so downstream of the weir, there is little public access to trout water below Carseland.

For many years the Blackfoot Indian band sold trespass permits to anglers who wished to fish the river through the reserve. This allowed people to float through the reserve and camp overnight before taking out at the Arrowwood bridge south of Gleichen. The practice also allowed anglers with motorboats to float down into the reserve and motor back out at the end of the day.

In the mid-1990s, however, the band stopped selling permits, which raised the contentious issue of who owns the riverbed. Most fly-fishers (and many lawyers) who have studied the situation are of the opinion that the riverbed below the high-water mark is public land and that anglers who stay below it are not trespassing. Some members of the band, nevertheless, maintain that the band retains ownership of the riverbed. For most anglers the lack of adequate access and the prospect of a less than warm reception are reasons enough to fish elsewhere.

It's possible that circumstances affecting access to the Bow on the Blackfoot Reserve will change as governments attempt to address aboriginal land claims. In the meantime anglers are best advised to check with Calgary flyshops to learn the current status of access to the Bow below Carseland.

The best access to the Bow River below the Bassano dam is from bridges on Highways 539, 36, 875 and 524. Permission from landowners is required to gain access at other points, which may prove difficult, since this is a big country with few people.

MIDDLE BOW FLIES
Dry Flies

Month	Fly	Size	Imitates
April 15– May 15 / August 15– October 15	Blue-Winged Olive Thorax	#18	*Baetis* mayflies
April 15– May 15 / August 15– October 15	Olive Floating Nymph	#16	*Baetis* mayflies

April 15– May 15 / August 15– October 15	Adams	#18	*Baetis* mayflies
May 15– June 15	March Brown / Adams	#14	March Brown mayflies
May 20– June 10	Brown Elk Hair Caddis	#12, 14	Caddisflies
June 15– July 25	Light Cahill / Pale Morning Spinner / Pale Morning Dun Thorax	#14, 16	Pale Morning Dun mayflies
June 15– September 30	Brown Elk Hair Caddis / LaFontaine Emergent Sparkle Pupa	#14–18	Caddisflies
July 20– September 20	Letort Hopper / Dave's Hopper / Stimulator	#6–10	Grasshoppers
August 1– October 15	Trico Thorax / Trico Spinner	#18, 20	*Tricorythodes* mayflies

Nymphs			
Month	Fly	Size	Imitates
All Season	San Juan Worm	#8–12	Aquatic worms

All Season	Bead-Head Prince	#10–14	Various mayflies
All Season	Gold-Ribbed Hare's Ear	#10–14	Various mayflies and stoneflies
All Season	Pheasant Tail	#12–16	Various mayflies
All Season	Yellow Stone	#4–8	Golden Stoneflies

Streamers			
Month	Fly	Size	Imitates
All Season	Clouser Minnow	#2–6	Minnows
All Season	Gander (olive or grey)	#2–6	Minnows
All Season	Bow River Bugger (olive or brown)	#2–6	Leeches and minnows
All Season	Woolly Bugger (olive, brown or white)	#2–8	Leeches and minnows

Note: Dates are approximate and will vary from year to year.

Fly Patterns

FOLLOWING are descriptions of some of my favorite Bow River flies. Those included here are by no means the only ones effective on the Bow, but they are the ones I have come to rely on over the years to provide the most consistent success. The streamers and nymphs are tied weighted because you can't go wrong by fishing too deep but you can by not fishing deep enough. Anglers should, however, note that flies tied with lead wire are prohibited in Banff National Park. Substitute materials are being developed.

STREAMERS

Woolly Bugger
(illustration page 169)

This is perhaps the best all-purpose streamer ever devised. It is commonly tied in olive and black, but it is effective in virtually all colors, including all black and all white. I believe it is the pulsing motion of the fly in the water that makes it successful rather than the color. Some tiers add rubber legs, lead eyes or flashabou.

HOOK: Mustad 79580 or 9672, or any long-shanked streamer hook, #2–8
WEIGHT: Lead wire
TAIL: Black marabou
BODY: Dark olive chenille
HACKLE: Black hackle, palmered
Note: Fly in photo is tied with a weed guard.

Gander
(illustration page 169)

This pattern was developed in the 1980s on the Bow River by Calgary flytier Mike Edgar. It has become one of the most popular streamers on the river and is tied in the grey version shown here as well as in olive.

HOOK: Mustad 79580 or any long-shanked streamer hook, #2–8
WEIGHT: Lead wire
TAIL: White marabou
BODY: Grey or olive mohair
RIB: Gold oval tinsel
WING: Natural grey-brown rabbit strip
COLLAR: Spun and clipped deer hair
HEAD: Sculpin wool (ram's wool), grey on top and white on bottom

Clouser Minnow
(illustration page 169)

This smallmouth bass fly from Pennsylvania is now being used to catch just about every gamefish that swims in fresh or saltwater. It is sparsely tied and sinks quickly, yet casts easily. Olive, brown and black are the favored colors for Bow River trout.

HOOK: Mustad 79580 or any long-shanked streamer hook, #2–8
OVERWING: Sparse olive, brown or black bucktail mixed with
pearl crystal flash
UNDERWING: Sparse white bucktail
LEAD EYES: Chrome, plain or painted
Note: The fly in illustration is tied inverted.

Bow River Bugger
(illustration page 169)

In the 1980s this fly was devised by guide Peter Chenier, who combined the best attributes of two great flies: the Woolly Bugger and the Muddler Minnow. It has since become the Bow's signature streamer. It can be tied in any combination of colors, but olive and brown are most popular.

HOOK: Mustad 79580 or any long-shanked streamer hook, #2–8
WEIGHT: Lead wire
TAIL: Black marabou mixed with a few strands of blue
flashabou
BODY: Olive chenille
HACKLE: Black hackle, palmered
COLLAR: Natural deer hair
HEAD: Spun and clipped white deer hair

NYMPHS

Bitch Creek
(illustration page 170)

This silly-looking fly is a popular pattern in Montana and is said to represent a large black stonefly nymph. I'm not convinced that it represents anything in particular, and though I'm embarrassed every time I tie one to a leader, I'm very convinced I should have some in my fly box. I find the Bitch Creek most effective when the water is a little high and a little discolored, and when I'm fishing from a drifting boat.

HOOK: Mustad 9672 or any 3X long nymph hook, #4, 6
WEIGHT: Lead wire
TAILS: Two strands of white rubber hackle
ABDOMEN: Black and orange chenille, woven, black on top
and orange on bottom
THORAX: Black chenille
HACKLE: Brown hackle, palmered over thorax
ANTENNAE: Two strands of white rubber hackle
Note: This pattern is usually tied heavily weighted.

Gold-Ribbed Hare's Ear
(illustration page 170)

Perhaps the most popular nymph in North America, this fly has
a place on the Bow. It may imitate some species of stonefly nymphs
when tied large and heavily weighted, or may represent emerging
mayflies or caddisflies when tied in smaller sizes.

HOOK: Mustad 9671 or any 2XL or 3XL nymph hook, #4–18
WEIGHT: Lead wire
TAIL: Hare's ear guard hairs
ABDOMEN: Hare's ear, dubbed
RIBBING: Gold wire or gold oval tinsel
THORAX: Hare's ear, dubbed thicker than abdomen with guard
hairs picked out
WING CASE: Mottled turkey

Pheasant Tail Nymph
(illustration page 170)

The original Pheasant Tail Nymph was devised by the English
river keeper Frank Sawyer. I find this variation particularly effective
for fish that are rising sporadically or that are visible in fairly shallow water. It may be tied with or without weight. A bead-head version is also very effective.

HOOK: Mustad 9671 or any 2XL nymph hook, #8–16

TAIL: Ring-necked pheasant tail fibers
ABDOMEN: Pheasant tail fibers, wrapped
RIBBING: Fine copper wire, reverse wrapped
THORAX: Peacock herl
WING CASE: Pheasant tail fibers
LEGS: Pheasant tail fibers

Yellow Stone Nymph
(illustration page 170)

Popularized by the late Charles Brooks, this is an imitation of the golden stonefly nymphs that are important on nearly every western river.

HOOK: Mustad 9672 or any 3XL nymph hook, #4–8
WEIGHT: Lead wire
TAIL: Two segments of mottled turkey
ABDOMEN: Medium brown yarn, overwrapped with dirty yellow yarn. The yellow yarn is tied in at the forward end of the abdomen and spiraled, palmer-style, back to the tail and then forward to the point it was tied in.
THORAX: Medium brown yarn
HACKLE: One grizzly and one grizzly dyed brown with the fibers stripped off one side. The two feathers are then wrapped together, forming two distinct bands of hackle, one at the rear of the thorax and the other in the center.
GILLS: Grey ostrich herl wrapped through the thorax exactly as hackle feathers were wrapped
RIBBING (OPTIONAL): Fine copper wire, reverse wrapped through abdomen and thorax

San Juan Worm
(illustration page 170)

I knew of the existence of aquatic worms on the Bow downstream of Calgary back in the late 1970s, but I didn't think they were important enough to imitate. Boy, was I wrong. This fly was originated on the San Juan River in New Mexico, but it has become a standard on the Bow and a number of other western rivers. This is just one of many variations of the pattern currently being used.

HOOK: Curved-shank nymph hook, #8–14
TAIL: Red floss
BODY: Flat, red monofilament (Cobra)

Bead-Head Prince
(illustration page 170)

The Prince Nymph has been a standard in the West for decades. It works well in the Bow in both its original and bead-head versions. I don't know what it imitates, but thankfully that troubles me more than it does the fish.

HOOK: Mustad 9671 or any 2XL or 3XL nymph hook, #8–14
BEAD: Brass, placed over hook shank and positioned at front of fly
TAILS: Two brown goose biots, tied split
BODY: Peacock herl
RIB: Medium gold oval tinsel
WINGS: Two white goose biots, tied down
HACKLE: Brown hen, tied soft-hackle style

DRY FLIES

Stimulator
(illustration page 171)

Versatility makes this a great fly to use on the upper and middle sections of the Bow through most of the summer. It is tied in a multitude of color combinations and can imitate a variety of stoneflies as well as grasshoppers.

HOOK: Mustad 94831 or any long-shanked dry-fly hook (sometimes tied on a curved-shank hook), #4–14
TAIL: Natural elk hair
ABDOMEN: Orange Fly Rite or Antron dubbing

REAR HACKLE: Short brown, palmered through abdomen
RIB: Fine gold or copper wire, reverse wrapped over rear
hackle
WING: Natural elk hair
THORAX: Yellow Fly Rite or Antron dubbing
FRONT HACKLE: Grizzly, palmered through thorax
HEAD: Fluorescent orange tying thread

Adams
(illustration page 171)

Because it can represent almost anything, the Adams is perhaps the single best dry fly in existence. It belongs in every angler's fly box.

HOOK: Mustad 94840 or any standard dry-fly hook, #14–20
TAIL: Grizzly and brown hackle fibers, mixed
BODY: Muskrat fur, dubbed
WINGS: Grizzly hackle tips
HACKLE: Grizzly and brown, mixed
Note: The Adams is sometimes tied with an olive body to match the Baetis *hatches.*

Blue-Winged Olive Thorax
(illustration page 171)

Thorax-style dry flies were shown to me by Leigh Perkins of the Orvis Company many years ago. Thorax flies are durable, easy to tie, land and float properly nearly every time and they catch fish. That leaves nothing out. They have become my favorite dry flies for imitating small- and medium-sized mayflies.

HOOK: Mustad 94840 or any light-wire dry-fly hook, #18, 20
TAIL: Blue dun hackle fibers, split
BODY: Olive fur or polypropylene dubbing
WING: One piece of dark grey turkey body feather, tied
upright in the center of the hook shank
HACKLE: Blue dun, wrapped to cover the center third of the
hook shank and trimmed flat on the bottom
THORAX: Olive fur or polypropylene dubbing

Elk Hair Caddis
(illustration page 171)

This universally popular adult caddis pattern was developed by Al Troth of Dillon, Montana.

HOOK: Mustad 94840 or any light-wire dry-fly hook, #12–18
BODY: Dubbed grey, brown or olive fur or polypropylene, palmered with grizzly or brown hackle
RIBBING: Very fine gold wire
WING: Elk hair (natural, bleached or dyed rusty brown)
HEAD: Butt ends of the elk hair wing

Olive Floating Nymph
(illustration page 172)

This is a fly devised by Rene Harrop for the selective rainbows of Idaho's Henry's Fork of the Snake. I find it a very good choice when the fish are feeding on the small *Baetis* mayflies in spring and autumn.

HOOK: Mustad 94840 or any light-wire dry-fly hook, #14–18
TAIL: Blue dun hackle fibers, tied split
BODY: Olive fur or polypropylene dubbing
WING CASE: Ball of grey polypropylene dubbing positioned on top of the hook shank
HACKLE: Blue dun hackle fibers, tied in two bunches, one on either side of the wing case

Letort Hopper
(illustration page 172)

Bob Scammell of Red Deer, Alberta, is the publicity chairman for this fly, and his diligence has resulted in the Letort becoming Alberta's favorite hopper pattern. Bob considers the standard pattern an imitation of both the grasshoppers and golden stoneflies that hatch on many western waters early in the summer. It also lends itself to variations through the substitution of different materials for wings. The variation shown here has pheasant tail fibers for legs.

HOOK: Mustad 94831 or any long-shanked dry-fly hook,
    #4–14
BODY: Yellow polypropylene or seal fur, dubbed
RIBBING: Brown rod-winding thread
WING: Section of mottled turkey, trimmed to shape and tied
    flat over the body
LEGS: Two bunches of knotted cock ring-necked pheasant tail
    fibers
COLLAR: Natural deer hair (on top and sides of fly only)
HEAD: Deer hair, spun and clipped

Pale Morning Dun Thorax
(illustration page 172)

This is my favorite imitation of the Pale Morning Dun.

HOOK: Mustad 94840 or any light-wire dry-fly hook, #16, 18
TAIL: Light blue dun hackle fibers, tied split
BODY: Creamy olive fur or polypropylene dubbing
WING: One piece of light grey turkey body feather, tied
    upright in the center of the hook shank
HACKLE: Light blue dun, wrapped to cover the center third of
    the hook shank and trimmed flat on the bottom
THORAX: Creamy olive fur or polypropylene dubbing

Pale Morning Spinner
(illustration page 172)

This very simple no-hackle fly is extremely useful for the frequent occasions when the fish feed on crippled duns during the
Pale Morning Dun hatch.

HOOK: Mustad 94840 or any light-wire dry-fly hook, #16
TAIL: Light blue dun hackle fibers, tied split
BODY: Creamy olive fur or polypropylene dubbing
WINGS: White polypropylene, tied spent

Green Paradrake
(illustration page 172)

The Western Green Drake is a very important insect on the upper Bow, hatching from mid-July to about mid-August, but it is not found downstream of Calgary. The Green Paradrake is just one of many good imitations of this big mayfly.

HOOK: Mustad 94840 or any light-wire dry-fly hook, #10, 12
TAIL: Several dark moose body hairs
BODY: Elk hair dyed olive, tied extended body-style
RIB: Yellow tying thread
WING: Dark grey deer hair
HACKLE: Grizzly dyed olive, tied parachute-style

LaFontaine Emergent Sparkle Pupa
(illustration page 172)

Gary LaFontaine of Deer Lodge, Montana, literally wrote the book on caddisflies. This pattern imitates the caddis pupa just as it is preparing to leave the water. Fish it in the film as you would a dry fly anytime caddisflies are abundant.

HOOK: Mustad 94840 or any light-wire dry-fly hook, #14–18
UNDERBODY: Dubbing made of brown yarn mixed and blended with brown fur
OVERBODY: Light brown Antron yarn pulled forward in a loose envelope to surround the body. A small piece of Antron yarn can be left as a trailing shuck.
WING: Light deer hair
HEAD: Brown fur, dubbed

9

The State of the Bow River Trout Fishery

THE BOW RIVER was largely a secret in international circles until the late 1970s, when some prominent anglers and outdoor writers sampled the river and began to spread the word. The first burst of publicity started in January 1979, when Leigh Perkins, owner of the Orvis Company, published an article describing his first visit to the Bow in the company's in-house publication, *The Orvis News*. Shortly thereafter articles on the newly discovered Bow appeared in *Sports Afield, Outdoor Life, Flyfishing the West, The Fly-Fisher* and *Fishing World* magazines. During the mid-1980s other magazine articles appeared in *Sports Afield, Field and Stream* and *Rod and Reel*. Lefty Kreh and Gary Borger produced videos dealing with the fly-fishing on the Bow, and numerous outdoor television programs produced features on it.

Public exposure made it impossible for the extraordinary quality of fly-fishing on the Bow River to remain unnoticed by anglers, and over the last two decades the river has become an increasingly popular stop on the international agenda. Ten of thousands of anglers have visited the river, and the number of guides and outfitters working the river has increased accordingly. Back in 1979 Russell Thornberry and Barry White were the only outfitters offering trips on the river and, other than me, there were only one or two full-time guides. The total number of guided trips taken that year was about 150. By 1986 the number of guided trips had increased tenfold, and the yearly total has remained in that range ever since. Vehicle shuttle services have similarly gotten busier. For example, Mike Guinn, who operates a shuttle service in conjunction with his Water Boatman guide business, told me that in 1998 his shuttle business alone had a "frequent client" list of 230 people, both guides and private anglers.

In recent years a great number of Calgarians have taken up fly-fishing on the Bow. Partly this is a result of the exposure recently given the sport in the media and in the film *A River Runs Through It,* and partly it's a result of people in cities looking for outdoor recreation close to home. It's now not at all unusual to see driftboats on trailers parked in driveways or rolling down Calgary's freeways throughout the summer.

The growing number of anglers on the Bow River has already made fishing more difficult. The river has long been thought of as one of intermediate difficulty, meaning that successful anglers must know the basics of where to find fish and how to present a fly properly. As the trout have been fished over more, they have become increasingly temperamental and require greater skill and adaptability on the part of anglers.

High fishing pressure is accepted fairly readily by visiting anglers but not so freely by local fly-fishers who were there in the good old days and who hope never to see traffic on the Bow as heavy as on many of the famed streams in the United States. It didn't bother me to find dozens of anglers on Pennsylvania's Yellow Breeches when I fished there, but it would definitely bother me to find the same number on my favorite stream at home. The Calgary locals—especially those who fished the river before it became famous—sometimes resent the presence of, as one fly-rodder put it to me, "a guide boat in every pool."

It's human nature to yearn for the good old days. Years ago the Bow produced exceptional numbers of huge fish, many to dry flies, and did so in nearly complete anonymity, except for a small group of dedicated anglers. We were aware of how unusual it was to have a fine trout stream flowing through a booming city, and we wondered about the fishery's chances for survival. We were living in the good old days, we knew it even then, and we wanted them to last. In one of the early magazine stories about the Bow, the late Keith Gardner wrote, "The world's best dry fly river isn't going to last forever."

Some among us were not optimistic about the Bow River's future. If someone had looked into a crystal ball 25 years ago and suggested that at the opening of the new millennium close to a million people would call the city of Calgary home, I probably would have believed it. But if I'd been told that Calgary would hold a million people *and* that the Bow River would still be a world-class trout stream, I'd have said we cheated fate. What is remarkable is not the fact that the fishery has changed but that it has changed so little. These may not be the good old days, but they're not bad either, considering all the fates that could have befallen the Bow.

Some local anglers would rather the river had remained a secret, but others of us are convinced international recognition will help ensure the Bow's survival as a premier trout stream. The publicity for the Bow ultimately prompted the Alberta government to recognize both the uniqueness of the fishery and its potential to provide monetary return to the province. Once it was apparent that there was something special about the Bow, attempts were made to gather information about it. Since then population and spawning studies have provided information useful to the intelligent management of the river. In all likelihood these studies would not have been conducted if the river had not captured the attention of the public.

Prior to 1983 the middle Bow, like most quality streams, underwent a series of gradually more restrictive bag limits. The limit, once as high as 20 fish per day, was reduced to 10 fish, then 5, then 5 fish with only 2 over 18 inches (46 cm) followed by 2 fish of any size. Population and spawning studies conducted during the 1980s provided the incentive for the more restrictive regulations that were placed on the river in 1983 between the Highway 22X bridge and the Carseland weir in an effort to prevent deterioration in the quality of the fishery. Designed to protect larger, mature fish of spawning age, the regulations require that all trout over 16 inches (40 cm) long be released unharmed and further specify a bag limit of two fish per day. In order to facilitate the successful release of captured fish, bait-fishing is not allowed.

The introduction of these regulations was a significant event in the life of the Bow River fishery, but it didn't come easily. Regional fisheries biologist Bill Griffiths had twice recommended more restrictive regulations on the river prior to 1981, but no changes were made. Once the new regulations were in place there was concern about how such restrictions, which were new to Alberta, would be received by the angling community. Some public resistance was anticipated, but in the end it was apparent to all that the regulations were in the best interest of the river.

In the spring of 1998 the provincial government introduced sweeping changes to the angling regulations on Alberta's eastern slopes trout streams. In general these regulations severely restrict the harvest of trout from moving waters. In the Bow from the Banff National Park boundary down to the Highway 22X bridge, bait cannot be used except in the autumn, and then only maggots are allowed. The upper river from the Banff park boundary to the Seebee dam has a zero limit on all trout except brook trout. The Highwood River, a major tributary of the Bow, is now regulated as a catch-and-release stream for all species but brook trout, and no fish may be killed after the end of August. As well, the Elbow River in the city of Calgary is closed to angling between October 1 and November 15 to protect spawning brown trout and whitefish. Alberta now leads the world in its efforts to protect wild trout, having placed 26 streams under complete catch-and-release regulations. The regulations have since been soundly applauded by anglers and biologists from around the world and have largely been accepted by the Alberta angling public.

GOOD NEWS

The river in Banff National Park is, by legislation, relatively safe from human tampering. No industry of any kind except tourism is carried out within the boundaries of the park. The town of Banff moved toward better stewardship of the upper Bow by installing a state-of-the-art municipal sewage treatment plant in the mid-1990s though overflow from the sewage lagoon at the Tunnel Mountain campground sometimes still enters the Cascade River untreated.

The river's life gets more complicated near Calgary. For both people and rivers there are certain dangers associated with life in a big city, and the Bow here leads a more precarious existence than isolated rivers. But while the city of Calgary presents the river with certain problems that don't affect back-country streams, it also provides the river with a multitude of concerned observers whose eyes are on it at all times. Consequently threats to its safety are usually discovered and identified early, and public pressure forces the city into corrective action. In November 1982, for instance, a fish kill affecting spawning brown trout and whitefish occurred in the Elbow River just below the Glenmore dam. Because the river flows through a popular city park, the problem was noticed and reported immediately by many citizens. Tests eventually showed that the source of the problem was chlorine used in the Glenmore water treatment plant. As a result dechlorinization equipment was quickly installed. If a problem of equal magnitude occurred on an isolated stream, it would likely remain undetected for some time, and public pressure to rectify it would not be as strong.

Public pressure over the last two decades has gradually compelled the city of Calgary to realize the value of the Bow River, both economically and esthetically, to its residents and visitors. Storm water from newer subdivisions is now collected and routed through man-made marshes, which naturally filter the water before it reaches the river. The city takes some pride in the fact that it is now a better steward of its river than many other cities.

Other good news for the Bow River watershed includes the provincial government's approval in 1998 of a storage reservoir project on the Little Bow River. If this project is executed under the conditions of its approval, it will benefit the Highwood River by catching and storing excess water in the spring and subsequently ensuring that more of it will be left in the river in the critical late summer period. The plan should make irrigators happy and improve the quality of the fishery, but the government has had a habit of over-allocating the water in its rivers, and the fear is that the habit may be hard to break.

Perhaps the best news of all regarding the future of the Bow River as a trout stream is the presence of Trout Unlimited Canada. Internationally Trout Unlimited has in excess of 100,000 members and a reputation for accomplishing its objectives of preserving or improving cold-water fish habitat. The organization has undergone tremendous growth in Alberta, from a total of about 60 members in 1984 to approximately 1,500 today. About 1,000 members belong to the Bow River Chapter in Calgary. Trout Unlimited's objectives in Alberta are to increase the profile of the province's angling resources, to make the public aware of the economic value of trout fishing, to initiate habitat projects and to work with government, business and other stakeholders to protect and enhance cold-water fish habitat. It also functions as a watchdog and lobby group regarding industrial activities that might affect the health of the river.

BAD NEWS

The Bow River system and the land through which it flows is controlled by a number of different parties: national parks, Indian bands, the city of Calgary and several towns, the Department of Environmental Protection, three irrigation districts and TransAlta Utilities. The Bow must serve many masters, and unfortunately they do not share the same objectives. For example, municipalities vary in their approach to development along rivers. The city of Calgary no longer permits urban development along the banks of the Bow and Elbow rivers, but rural municipalities in southern Alberta have no such restriction. In the town of High River, for instance, housing and golf course developments have been permitted on the banks of the Highwood River. Inevitably the river will flood (the name of the town is *High* River, after all), property owners will lobby hard to riprap or channelize the river to prevent a recurrence and the fishery will be permanently harmed. No coherent approach to river management can be developed until all parties can agree to a uniform set of regulations.

Power production remains a problem on parts of the Bow and its tributaries. The severe variation in flow volume caused by hydro dams between the Banff National Park boundary and the Bearspaw dam is the single largest factor limiting the quality of the upper Bow River fishery and inhibiting recreational use of the river. Fluctuating water levels create a biological dead zone along the riverbank, severely limit invertebrate life and fish productivity, and generally make the river unpredictable and at times even unsafe for recreational use. An encouraging sign in this regard is that after much discussion with the Jumpingpound Chapter of Trout Unlimited Canada, TransAlta Utilities, which produces the power, seems willing to give river stability a higher priority in its management of the river.

One river that could have benefited from such an approach to resource management in the past is the Kananaskis River, which was once a fine trout stream but which was ruined as a fishery by power dams. Much of the river's productivity as a fishery could still be restored if a re-regulation dam were built. The idea has circulated for years to build a small, inexpensive dam with the purpose of stabilizing the river, much as the Bearspaw dam does on the Bow. Though the idea is not dead it is still nothing more than talk and is no closer to reality than it was over a decade ago.

The most serious problems the Bow River will face in the future are related to the city of Calgary, to its industry and to agriculture in southern Alberta. To counter the continuing cycle of municipal growth followed by deteriorating water quality, the city will need to make upgrading its municipal sewage treatment capabilities a high priority early in the new century. Industry continues to pose threats to the river's welfare as well. Wildlife kills attributed to industrial discharges have occurred as recently as the winter of 1985–86, when more than 100 ducks died as a result of mysterious oil slicks that appeared in side channels of the river in Calgary. The determined efforts of such groups as Trout Unlimited will be needed to make industries increasingly aware of the favorable public opinion that can result only from conscientiously safeguarding the river.

Considerable additional stress will continue to be placed on the Bow River watershed by the agriculture industry, which is the mother of all water users in Alberta. The province's irrigation system accounts for 80 percent of all water use in Alberta and in 1985 accounted for 34 percent of all water used in Canada.

In the 1980s the greatest fear of recreational users of the Bow River was the prospect of a huge dam and irrigation storage reservoir on the mainstem river a few miles downstream of Calgary. Such a dam was part of a provincial government plan to transfer water from northern Alberta, where there is plenty of water but few people, to southern Alberta, where the reverse is true. The prospect of such a project was a fearsome specter for people who love rivers. Thankfully the idea, if not dead, has at least remained dormant for a number of years. The province is now unlikely to fund such megaprojects, and dams have lost some luster in the eyes of the North American public in recent years.

Currently the biggest danger from irrigation is that more water is sometimes taken from the river and its tributaries than the system can endure, especially in dry years. The resulting low water levels cause high water temperatures, low dissolved oxygen levels and dead fish. The two diversion intakes for irrigation on the Highwood River, one in the town of High River and one west of the town at Squaw Coulee, have been among the worst offenders. At the High River site, in the summer of 1984, a gravel deflector was installed so that as much as 50 percent of the Highwood River could be diverted into the Little Bow River system for irrigation. Flows in the Highwood were reduced to 72 cubic feet (2 m³) per

second by one department of government—Alberta Environment—after a minimum of 150 cubic feet (4.4 m^3) per second was
recommended by another department—the Fish and Wildlife
Division. The reduced volume of water quickly warmed, dense
plant growth occurred and lethal dissolved oxygen deficiencies
resulted. A fish kill occurred in August 1984 that affected an estimated 1,850 whitefish. Public protest was heard, but the official
reaction from the Department of Environment was that it was a
"minor" kill and that the heavy withdrawal of water from the
Highwood River was a response to an "emergency" situation in the
agriculture industry. It took five years of diligent effort on the part
of conservationists, but eventually temporary emergency regulations were put in place to ensure that an adequate volume of water
would be left in the Highwood. This has improved conditions for
the juvenile fish that migrate down to the Bow from the Highwood and Sheep River systems in midsummer, but a decade later
the regulation governing minimum flows in the Highwood River
is still not permanent.

Additional problems exist at the Carseland weir, where fish
move into the irrigation canal through the summer only to die
when the water is shut off each autumn. It is believed that many
of these fish would otherwise continue downstream over the weir
to take up residence in the Bow below Carseland. This problem
was pointed out to me in 1986 by both regional biologist Bill
Griffiths and John Eisenhauer, the former executive director of the
Bow River Chapter of Trout Unlimited Canada. In recent years
volunteers from the Bow River Chapter have conducted a fish rescue each fall, catching them in the canal and moving them back to
the river before the flow is shut off. In 1997 volunteers returned
16,000 trout and whitefish to the Bow. In 1998 the fish rescue
returned 90,000 trout and whitefish. Their efforts have helped
focus attention on the huge number of fish that have been lost to
the canal each year. It is hoped that a mechanical or electronic
means of keeping trout from entering the canal will be proposed
shortly. Thankfully one of the conditions specified in the approval
of the Little Bow reservoir project was the future use of fish-exclu-

sion devices there and at all other irrigation diversions. Let's hope that the means and money to retrofit existing diversions are found soon. The Carseland weir also fragments the continuity of the fishery downstream of Calgary. A fish ladder at the weir is supposed to provide fish an upstream route around the weir, but the ladder is poorly designed and doesn't work properly. Fish can make their way safely downstream over the weir, but they cannot use the ladder to return unless the river is flowing at more than 5,000 cubic feet (146 m^3) per second. The Alberta Fish and Wildlife Division has been aware of this problem since 1971, but to date no corrective action has been taken. A solution would finally provide for fish migration in both directions, which will integrate the trout population in the river and benefit the fishery both above and below the weir.

Another potential problem at Carseland involves the Alberta Department of Environmental Protection, which, as owner and operator of the weir, has begun to enlarge the canal that carries water out of the Bow for irrigation. The department is being pressed by the Alberta River Conservation Foundation to conduct an environmental impact study of the project, but the department is resisting, presumably because it knows that such a study would recommend against enlarging the weir.

Below the Bassano dam the problem gets worse as yet more Bow River water is diverted for irrigation. Unfortunately the Eastern Irrigation District's license only requires that 100 cubic feet (3 m^3) per second of water be left in the Bow below Bassano, even when the Bow at Calgary may be discharging over 3,000 cubic feet (87 m^3) per second. Fish kills are known to have occurred in this part of the river when the flow is severely reduced.

We can expect more struggles over Bow River water in the future as the Western Irrigation District, which operates the diversion weir in the city of Calgary, attempts to regain 460,000 acre feet (56,140 ha m) of Bow River water to which it claims it is entitled. This volume is described as "unused" water and also is coveted by the city of Calgary, TransAlta Utilities and the Eastern Irrigation District. A frightening prospect is the possibility that the three irrigation districts on the Bow may begin to pool their resources and cooperate to ensure that no Bow River water escapes "unused."

Beyond protecting the quality of the Bow River fishery, effort must be made to preserve the quality of the angling experience the river offers. Currently in Alberta fishing guides are not licensed, so anyone may simply purchase a business license, put an advertisement in a magazine and declare himself a guide. This is disturbing for two reasons. First, it allows unqualified people to offer "guided" trips on the river. When anglers entrust themselves to inexperienced guides, their trip may be unsatisfactory at best or their safety may be jeopardized at worst. Second, it allows an unlimited number of guides and outfitters to work the river, diminishing the experience for all anglers, guided or otherwise. Someday it may prove necessary to place a daily limit on the number of guide boats on the river, but I don't know how such a number could be chosen and who would have the authority to enforce it to the benefit of some and the detriment of others. I do know that some of the most experienced and knowledgeable guides anywhere work on the Bow, but in the present circumstances they are obliged to share their river and their livelihood with some who are less than adequately qualified.

Both these problems could be partially addressed through the provincial licensing of fishing guides. Qualifications should be stringent and should require that candidates have had a good deal of fishing experience on the Bow River, that they demonstrate a high degree of boating skills, that they be qualified in first aid, that they prove financial responsibility and that they carry adequate insurance. Such regulations would help limit the number of guides on the river to those genuinely experienced and qualified.

As Calgary's population and wealth continue to grow the use of high-speed boats and jet skis on the Bow will become an increasingly contentious issue. Large numbers of powerboats and large numbers of fly-fishers generally do not mix well. The boats disturb fish and occasionally endanger wading anglers. Though motors are no longer permitted on the river within the city, they are allowed elsewhere on the river. Some are used by anglers and some by people who simply want a place to drive their boat in spite of a number of nearby lakes better suited to high-speed boating. Should powerboat traffic continue to increase on the Bow, visiting anglers will be turned off (to say nothing of local fly-fishers) such that they will never come back, and the Bow's value as an economic resource will be diminished. Two possible solutions would be a regulation restricting horsepower or a total ban on powerboats on the river between Banff and Carseland.

In spite of progressive new angling regulations for Alberta's eastern slopes streams, Bow River brown trout are still exposed to harvest during spawning season. The portions of both the Elbow River and the Bow within the city of Calgary are important spawning areas for Bow River browns. Beginning in 1998 the Elbow was closed to angling each autumn, but only a small portion of the Bow in Calgary has been similarly closed. Mature brown trout downstream of the Highway 22x bridge are protected from harvest, but protected only until they migrate upstream into the city in preparation to spawn. How wise is it to protect them all year but then expose them to harvest when they begin to prepare for the most important job they have? An autumn closure, or at least an autumn no-kill regulation on brown trout within the city, seems a prudent idea.

All the regulations in the world, however, will not protect the fishery if a parasitic infection found in trout streams of the western United States makes its way into the Bow. Called Whirling Disease because of the behavior exhibited by infected trout fry, it has severely reduced the population of wild rainbow trout in the Madison River and other treasured American trout streams. Little has been known about this disease until very recently, but it has become apparent that it can be spread from one watershed to another via the transfer of dead fish, hatchery fish, or water or mud from infected streams. We don't know where this trail will lead, but study must continue, and anglers must be diligent to ensure that the infection is not transferred into Alberta streams.

A constant problem facing the groups that work to protect Alberta's natural resources is the chronic shortage of funding. Funding to the Fish and Wildlife Division was cut well beyond the bone in the 1980s, and the effect is now witnessed in a multitude of fish, wildlife and environmental matters. There hasn't been a population study on the Bow since 1992 or an economic evaluation of the river since 1988. New studies are needed to measure the benefits of current regulations and to point the way toward further conservation efforts. Let's hope that better economic times will result in an increase in funding.

Even fly-fishers themselves may eventually pose a threat to the Bow River trout fishery if the number of anglers on the river continues to grow at its present pace into the twenty-first century. It is believed there is a point at which incidental kill from catch-and-release angling (estimated at 5–10 percent by most experts) can become significant to a healthy fish population though no one knows at what stage it affects a fishery.

Another troubling matter is the fact that Alberta has a history of reacting to fish and wildlife problems only when they reach the crisis stage. Preventative medicine has not often been prescribed. The provincial ban on the harvest of bull trout, the sweeping new regulations for eastern slopes streams, the walleye recovery program and the study of the collapsed northern pike fisheries in northern Alberta have all been positive steps, but action was only taken at the eleventh hour (or maybe later).

So what is a river like the Bow worth and why should we bother to save it? The main problem with the question is that, even though rivers transcend financial evaluation, the world is driven by financial evaluations. The future health of our rivers is unfortunately entrusted to political decisions made by politicians rather than biological decisions made by biologists. Make no mistake, the biologists know exactly what it will take to preserve the Bow. Unfortunately the politicians listen frequently to powerful lobby groups and rarely to biologists. Political decisions are always concerned with the short-term future, while environmental decisions must be concerned with the long-term.

In September 1985 Calgary angler Neil Jennings, who has long been at the forefront of preserving and protecting the Bow River, was a guest speaker for a chapter of Trout Unlimited Canada. He addressed the issue thus:

> *Let's assume that we go to talk to a politician and propose to him that we are going to promote an industry in his constituency. This industry requires little or no capital expenditure to sustain it. It is based on an inventory which is relatively cost free and which is self-perpetuating and self-renewable. Cash returns from the industry will benefit hotels, transportation rentals, food outlets, a myriad of service establishments and will create employment in the general area. The industry is very cost-effective and will continue to spin off economic benefits on a perpetual basis if it receives a modicum of governmental regulation to protect it. The governmental expenses related to the industry will be moderate at worst, and some of the government's expense will be offset by people who will do business with the industry. The industry will not be a nuisance to other industries in the constituency and will not appreciably denigrate the other industries in the constituency. If you put this concept to any politician, he would think that you have brought him a miracle. Well, you have. You have brought him a trout stream.*

Neil Jennings' comments point to a fundamental truth of the contemporary political experience. These days if one hopes to convince people that something is valuable, it must have a dollar sign attached to it. In 1988 a study concluded that the Bow River was worth $11–$13 million annually to the city of Calgary. Of this total about $5 million came directly from anglers, both local and visiting. The value of the river has increased dramatically since, and a 1998 estimate from Trout Unlimited Canada put the angler's contributions at $20–$25 million annually.

I have used angling as a measure of the river's economic value because it is more easily monitored than other recreational pursuits, but fishing is just one of many reasons people are drawn to the Bow. Canoeists, kayakers, hikers, campers, cyclists, photographers, hunters, bird watchers, mountain climbers and a host of others come here partly or wholly because of the fabulous recreational resource that exists in and around the Bow Valley.

What need we do to preserve the future of the Bow River? As

I see it we must continue to make our politicians aware of the economic value of the river. We must take into account the operating principle of the politicians, and we must convince them that enough of us are concerned with the future of the Bow to jeopardize their chances of reelection. If we accomplish these two things we may find that the preservation of the Bow River receives a higher priority than fish and wildlife matters have traditionally had in Alberta.

While focusing our efforts on educating politicians and the public on the value of the Bow, we can't underestimate the value of its tributaries. A river and its tributaries are a web with a multitude of influences upon one another. Protection of the critical spawning tributaries from overgrazing and clear-cut logging must be ensured, and the agriculture industry must be made aware that recreational river use and irrigation *can* coexist. One need not be sacrificed for the other. Among the most urgently needed regulations is the enacting of minimum flow regulations for the Bow below Carseland.

The protective angling regulations on the middle Bow River must stay in place to ensure that the increasing fishing pressure on the river doesn't harm the fish population.

We must see a change of attitude within the Fish and Wildlife Division, which through the 1990s has seemed to act as though the welfare of the Bow River, after being in the spotlight through the 1980s, could be relegated to a lower priority. The Bow fishery must be monitored more frequently to determine its state of health, including continued testing for Whirling Disease. More frequent population studies must be done, and a new economic evaluation of the river must be undertaken. The latter is critical, for it would provide great incentive to initiate all the other protective steps.

Finally groups like Trout Unlimited must be supported more than morally. They deserve our time and money.

Sometimes I visit "my river" without any tackle or any intention of fishing. Thirty years spent on the river have softened the need to partake at every opportunity, and I go simply because I need to know that all is in order. Such times reinforce to me that the value of the Bow River goes beyond even the significance of rising fish and the chance to catch a big one.

In the final analysis the value of a river, like any wild thing, is beyond the realm of financial measures. The most compelling attraction of the Bow River for me and many, many others is in the simple opportunity it affords us to completely and utterly lose ourselves. We can cast a fly, paddle a canoe or simply sit beside the river for a day without once concerning ourselves with things that are not so much genuinely important as they are temporarily urgent. The phone doesn't ring. You don't need a daytimer. In my life it has been the Bow River's role to deliver me from such urgency, and for that I am grateful. Few things in life can accomplish as much.

If this book leaves you with a single lasting impression I hope it is that the Bow is a unique river in a unique situation. It is the only world-class trout stream that flows through a major metropolitan center, and its quality today is largely the consequence of good fortune we can no longer rely upon. How the Bow River fares into the new millennium will be the result of our efforts to intelligently manage and passionately protect it.

Bibliography

Alberta Business Development and Tourism. *Reach Reports of the South Saskatchewan River System.* Edmonton: Alberta Business Development and Tourism, n.d.

Alberta Energy and Natural Resources. *Status of the Fish and Wildlife Resource in Alberta.* Edmonton: Alberta Energy and Natural Resources, 1984.

Alberta Department of the Environment. *Water Quality: Bow River 1972–1973.* Calgary: Department of the Environment, 1974.

Alberta Department of the Environment, Water Resources Division. *City of Calgary Flood Study, Volume One, Bow River Report.* Calgary: City of Calgary, 1973.

Alberta Environment. *Summary Report South Saskatchewan River Basin Planning Program.* Edmonton: Alberta Environment, 1984.

Alberta Environmental Health Services Division, Water Pollution Control Section, Department of Health. *Fish Kill in the Bow River During the Week of August 28, 1967.* Calgary: Government of Alberta, n.d.

Appleby, Edna (Hill). *Canmore: The Story of an Era.* Calgary: n.p., 1975.

Brooks, Charles E. *The Living River.* Garden City: Doubleday & Company, 1979.

Calgary Power, Royal Commission on Flooding. *Ice Conditions on the Bow River.* Calgary: Calgary Power, 1963.

Foran, Max. *Calgary: An Illustrated History.* Toronto: James Lorimer & Company and National Museum of Man, 1978.

Friesen. *The Arrowwood Story.* Arrowwood: Farm Women's Union of Alberta, Arrowwood Local, 1964.

Gordon, Sid W. *How to Fish from Top to Bottom.* Stackpole Books, 1978.

Helfrich, H. *Physical, Chemical and Biological Features of the Bow*

River:A Literature Review. Calgary:Alberta Department of Energy and Natural Resources, 1980.

Hildebrand, L. and G. Ash. *A Fish Harvest Survey on the Bow River, Alberta.* Edmonton: R.L. & L. Environmental Services, 1982.

Hocking, Anthony. *Alberta.* Toronto: McGraw-Hill Ryerson, 1979.

Huck, Barbara. *In Search of Ancient Alberta.* Winnipeg: Heartland Publications, 1998.

Hutchison, Bruce. *The Fraser.* Toronto: Clarke, Irwin & Co., 1950.

Kellerhals, R., C.R. Neill and D.I. Bray. *Hydraulic and Geomorphic Characteristics of Rivers in Alberta.* Edmonton:Alberta Cooperative Research Program in Highway and River Engineering, 1972.

Kelly, Michael L. *Attitudes Toward the Environment: A Comparison of Six Surveys Spanning Six Years.* Edmonton: Environment Council of Alberta, 1982.

Kussat, Rick H. *Studies on Certain Ecological Aspects of the Bow River.* Calgary: Division of Fish and Wildlife Alberta, Department of Lands and Forests, n.d.

Lewis, Margaret. *To Conserve a Heritage.* Edmonton: Alberta Fish and Game Association, 1979.

Luxton, Eleanor G. *Banff, Canada's First National Park.* Banff: Summerthought, 1975.

MacDonald, Janice E. *Canoeing Alberta.* Edmonton: Lone Pine Publishing, 1985.

MacGregor, J.G. *A History of Alberta.* Edmonton: Hurtig Publishers, 1972.

McDonald, Dennis G. *A Preliminary Assessment of the Impact of the Carseland Dam Reconstruction Upon Fish, Wildlife and Recreation Resource Potentials of the Lower Bow River Valley With Recommendations for Impact Amelioration.* Edmonton: Faculty of Graduate Studies, University of Calgary, 1975.

———. *Rainbow Trout and Canada Goose Reproduction Relative to Existing and Predicted Post-Impoundment Conditions in the Bow River Basin, Alberta.* Calgary: Faculty of Graduate Studies, University of Calgary, 1975.

McIllree, J.H. and M.H.White-Fraser. "Fishing in Southern Alberta." *Alberta History.* Vol. 3, No. 2 (Spring 1983).

Nature's Lifeline: Prairie and Northern Rivers. Calgary: Canada West Foundation, 1982.

Nielsen, C.V., ed. *Bowness Golden Jubilee.* Calgary: Historical Committee of the Golden Jubilee, n.d.

Paetz, Martin J. and Joseph S. Nelson. *The Fishes of Alberta.* Edmonton: Government of Alberta, 1970.

Rawson, D.S. *Biological Investigations on the Bow and Kananaskis Rivers in 1947.* Calgary: Calgary Power, 1948.

Report of the Select Committee on Recreational and Commercial Fishing Industries in Alberta. 1980.

Sosiak, A.J. and W.E. Griffiths. *Bow River Trout Population Studies Fall 1980–82.* Calgary: Fish and Wildlife Division, Alberta Energy and Natural Resources, 1984.

———. *Bow River Rainbow Trout Spawning Surveys Spring 1983–84.* Calgary: Fish and Wildlife Division, Alberta Energy and Natural Resources, 1984.

———. *Elbow and Bow River Brown Trout Spawning Surveys Fall 1982.* Calgary: Fish and Wildlife Division, Alberta Energy and Natural Resources, 1983.

Spalding, David A.E., ed. *A Nature Guide to Alberta.* Edmonton: Hurtig Publishers, 1980.

Stelfox, J.D. and R.D. Konynenbelt. *An Inventory of Fish Populations and Fish Habitat in the Elbow River and Fish Creek Watersheds.* Calgary: Fish and Wildlife Division, Alberta Energy and Natural Resources, 1980.

Stelfox, J.D. *Bow River Spawning Channels Fall Spawning Study.* Calgary: Fish and Wildlife Division, Alberta Energy and Natural Resources, 1979.

Strong, W.L. and K.R. Leggat. *Ecoregions of Alberta.* Edmonton: Alberta Energy and Natural Resources, 1981.

The Hydro and Hydro-Electric Energy Potential of Alberta: A Preliminary Appraisal. Calgary: Alberta Energy Resources Conservation Board, 1973.

Thompson, G.E. *Bow River Creel Census (1977).* Edmonton: Alberta Fish and Wildlife, 1978.

Ward, J.C. *The Fishes and Their Distribution in the Mountain National Parks of Canada*. Calgary: Canadian Wildlife Service, 1974.

Wiebe, A.P. and R.D. Konynenbelt. *Spawning Survey, Habitat Utilization, and Fish Distribution, Bow River, 1980*. Calgary: Fish and Wildlife Division, Alberta Energy and Natural Resources, 1980.

Wilson, Michael. *Once Upon a River: Archaeology and Geology of the Bow River Valley at Calgary, Alberta, Canada*. Ottawa: National Museums of Canada, 1983.

Trout Streams of Alberta
A Guide to the Best Fly-Fishing

Among fly-fishers, Alberta is fast becoming known as a special place where anglers can find a lifetime of sport. Veteran fly-fisher Jim McLennan examines his home province drainage by drainage, focusing on the best opportunities that each provides—from wilderness cutthroat and grayling streams to intimate brown trout creeks to internationally acclaimed rainbow rivers. Jim McLennan draws on thirty years of fly-fishing experience to make sound recommendations on tackle, technique and fly patterns. The presentation is enhanced by detailed maps, color and black and white illustrations, hatch charts and profiles of each Alberta trout species. Written in an engaging, personal style, this is a book anglers will refer to frequently for vital information and will return to just as often for pleasure.

Also by Jim McLennan

"This book contains everything you need to know about fly-fishing for trout in Alberta's waters. Every fly-fisher from novice to veteran stands to learn a great deal—and have a lot of fun in the process." –Bruce Masterman, Outdoor Writer, *Calgary Herald*

"Trout Streams of Alberta is a delightful read and almost as good as fishing with the man in person. It will teach you how to find great fishing places." –Bob Scammell, author, *The Phenological Fly*

"Jim McLennan is one of Canada's fly-fishing treasures, a writer who captures the beauty, passion and excitement of Western Canada's trout fishing waters. I guarantee that after reading this book you'll want to cast a fly in his beloved waters—the last trout fishing frontier." –Jack Dennis, Jackson Hole, Wyoming, author, *Jack Dennis' Western Fly Tying Manual*

Bow River Nymphs and Streamers

Woolly Bugger

Gander

Clouser Minnow

Bow River Bugger

Bitch Creek

Gold-Ribbed Hare's Ear

Pheasant Tail Nymph

Yellow Stone Nymph

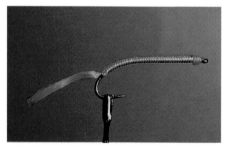

San Juan Worm

Bead-Head Prince

Bow River Dry Flies

Stimulator

Adams

Blue-Winged Olive Thorax

Elk Hair Caddis

Olive Floating Nymph

Letort Hopper

Pale Morning Dun Thorax

Pale Morning Spinner

Green Paradrake

LaFontaine Emergent Sparkle Pupa

A Year on the Bow
A Photo Essay

A September afternoon on the Bow below Calgary.

The Upper Bow River

Lake Louise, near the headwaters of the Bow—one of the most photographed alpine scenes in the world.

Winter on the upper Bow near Mount Yamnuska.

A brown trout typical of the upper Bow.

A driftboat trip on the upper Bow near Canmore.

A summer day on the Bow near Banff.

Fishing a side channel of the upper Bow in winter.

Knee-deep in fly-fishing heaven on the Bow below Banff.

The Middle Bow River

Lynda McLennan nets a rainbow near Calgary.

A glorious autumn day on the middle Bow just below Calgary.

A silver rainbow from
the Bow below Calgary.

Solitude, serenity and sunset on the middle Bow.

Stalking the flats on the middle Bow on an autumn afternoon.

A brown trout returning to its element.

Late summer hopper fishing. The Bow is a big river that can have small-stream appeal.

Casting to holding water on the banks of the middle Bow.

The Lower Bow River

Pronghorn antelope
near Brooks.

The lower Bow has changed little from the river Crowfoot would have known.

The Grand Forks where the Bow meets the Oldman River.

A goldeye from the lower Bow.